West Academic
Emeritus Advisory Board

a short & happy guide to
Conquering the MBE

Don L. Doernberg
Professor of Law Emeritus
Pace University Elisabeth Haub School of Law
Sometimes Visiting Professor of Law
University of the Pacific McGeorge School of Law

Cynthia A. Pope
Member, California and New York Bars

A SHORT & HAPPY GUIDE® SERIES

WEST
ACADEMIC
PUBLISHING

a short & happy guide series is a trademark registered in the U.S. Patent and Trademark Office.

© 2021 LEG, Inc. d/b/a West Academic

    444 Cedar Street, Suite 700
    St. Paul, MN 55101
    1-877-888-1330

Printed in the United States of America

ISBN: 978-1-64708-837-8

About the Authors

Don was on the full-time faculty at Pace University School of Law from 1979 to 2016. He has taught Civil Procedure, Conflict of Laws, Criminal Law, Criminal Procedure, Federal Courts, Torts, and the Law of Church and State. When he left Pace in 2016, Cyndy and he moved to California, and where for a few years he was Sometimes Visiting Professor at University of the Pacific McGeorge School of Law.

Upon graduation from law school, Cyndy was in-house counsel for IBM for nine years but then decided that she wanted to be a full-time mom. That turned out to be very fortunate, because we have a child with special needs. We became quite familiar with Special-Education Law and conducted a limited practice, representing children who required services under the Individuals with Disabilities in Education Act (IDEA) or accommodations under the Americans with Disabilities Act (ADA), taking all cases *pro bono*. We also became Parent Members of our school district's Committee on Special Education and served in that capacity for about fifteen years.

Both of us are members of the New York and California bars.

Don Doernberg
Cyndy Pope

December, 2020

Table of Contents

A Short & Happy Guide to Conquering the MBE

Prologue

One of the hoops you must jump through to become a licensed attorney in the United States is the Multistate Bar Examination. It takes up a day of states' two-day bar examinations[1] (though some states count it as somewhat less than 50% of the score). It ostensibly examines in seven areas: Civil Procedure, Constitutional Law, Contracts, Criminal Law, Evidence, Property, and Torts. Realize, however, that Constitutional Law also takes in some areas that most law schools would characterize as Federal Courts or Criminal Procedure, and Criminal Law may include procedure questions as well.

There are two possibilities with respect to the MBE: you can conquer it, or it can conquer you. We recommend the former. We present here a study method we adopted in 1985 when we were studying for the California Bar Examination. It was the second bar examination (no, no, not the second *try*) for each of us; we were already admitted in New York. Don is so old he had never even seen an MBE; it did not exist when he took the bar in New York. Cyndy took the New York Bar Examination in 1983. When her in-house-

---

[1] A few states have a partial third day.

counsel job at IBM moved to California, she had to take the California test because, unlike many other states, California requires that all in-house counsel take the California examination irrespective of how many other states' bars they may belong to.[2]

As we were preparing, we began to use practice multiple-choice questions as review and study tools rather than simply as assessment tools. Most students use practice questions simply to "see how they are doing"—as summative assessment. It seems to be a separate process from actually reviewing and studying subject matter, but it need not be—indeed, it *should not* be. Practice questions, done properly, are not just evaluation tools, they are indispensable *study* tools. This also makes them less intimidating, which brings us to a caution.

Students often characterize themselves as "terrible at multiple-choice questions." And they repeat that to themselves, over and over again, in various ways. That is not helpful; in fact, it is destructive. It is misdirected psychological conditioning that simply reinforces that particular feeling of inadequacy. Don't do that to yourself. If multiple-choice questions have been a challenge for you in the past, fair enough. But don't project it into the future; that's just talking yourselves out of being able to become proficient.[3] We designed this book to teach you how to become proficient.

---

[2]   Don did not have to take the examination at all but decided to (1) mostly to keep Cyndy company and (2) but secondarily to see the examination his students were encountering. He is a bit of a masochist.

[3]   Just think of how you would react if, when you are approaching an important challenge, someone else followed you around, reminding you every few moments how awful you are at whatever skill is involved. How long would it take before you at least felt like taking a swing at that person? (We trust you would not indulge the feeling—think "Torts.") Well, it's even worse when you are the source of the unpleasant communication. When someone else says something derogatory about us, we can always simply tell ourselves that that person is an idiot. When we think derogatory things about ourselves, it's really quite difficult to write that off as coming from someone who knows nothing. You would never permit someone else to do that to you, and that's fine. But it's even more important that *you* not do that to you.

Please do keep in mind that we seek to present here a system of study for the MBE. It is to prepare you to get the most out of your studying by using multiple-choice questions as study tools. It is not a substitute for doing practice examinations under examination conditions, but we hope you will find it effective as a method of substantive review for both the practice examinations and for the Main Event.

CHAPTER 1

Getting the MBE in Perspective

The MBE is the most controllable part of the bar examination. Different states test different numbers of subjects on their non-MBE days. California, for example, examines on thirteen subjects; seven of those are the MBE subjects. Pennsylvania, on the other hand adds another nine subjects, including state law in several areas that also appear on the MBE. Illinois adds thirteen subjects to the MBE's seven. It is easy to feel overwhelmed by the sheer number of subjects, and that is where the MBE comes in. It can be your insurance policy, because if you do well enough on the MBE, you have "room," as it were, to make errors on the other day of the examination without endangering your chances of passing.

We suggest that you approach multiple-choice questions differently from the way most of us learned to do them, and that may make you uncomfortable at first. For that and one other important reason, we urge you to begin practicing this technique very early—as early as your first year in law school (in your copious free time). At first the technique is slow going, and you may find yourself thinking that you would never have time to do it this way on the MBE. Not so! There is no denying that the technique is slow at first, but then, reading cases and studying is slow at first also. With lots of practice, the technique becomes much more rapid, so rapid that you can do it on the examination and finish. When you find yourself going very slowly at the beginning, remember that you are actually studying the material as you do it, not taking an examination against time.

It is a bit like beginning to learn to play tennis.[1] At the outset, you have to learn how to get into position for each kind of shot, how to stand to hit each kind of shot, how to swing for each kind of shot, and how to get yourself back in position to receive the next shot (and you cannot wait until your opponent strikes the ball to do that). That's a lot to keep in mind all at the same time. It is very slow at the beginning, and there is no way that most of us can participate in anything resembling a rally until we have lots and lots of practice at each individual stroke, usually with a teacher feeding balls to us so that we practice the same stroke over and over again. But as it becomes more familiar, it gets easier and more fluid. That does not happen overnight, but it does happen, and suddenly all those different components you used to have to think about individually to strike the ball successfully begin to meld; they become second nature.

There is another aspect to this technique as well. Studying abstract principles of law does not get you very far. You have to use them. Take our tennis example. You can read everything anyone has ever written about tennis, especially the how-to books. You can even memorize them, but your body still won't know how to play tennis. Don used to be a Red Cross Water Safety Instructor. He can tell you more about how to swim properly than any reasonable person would want to know, but you still won't know how to swim.

---

[1]   Or, really, any other sport, whether team or individual.

You have to get in the water. Using practice multiple-choice questions the way we suggest is getting into the water.

Most of us learned to do multiple-choice questions in a way that does not work well when the subject is law. Most multiple-choice examinations test little more than your accumulation of information. There's a question, some possible answers, and you look for the one that is correct.[2] There's nothing wrong with that in your earlier years of school, but as you go through the years, your teachers expect more of you, and the questions become more difficult. As you know by now, studying law is not primarily accumulation of information; it is learning how to work with information—with facts and law, how to get to at least a tentative answer when you are not sure, how to make arguments for or against a position, and how the courts are likely to react to the arguments. It is distinctly *not* about how many things you can remember.[3]

On the other hand, if you use multiple-choice questions as study tools, you will remember principles of law much better, and you'll be able to apply them to real situations. So how does all of this come about?

---

[2] Educational-testing experts call the alternatives that are not correct "distractors," and the goal for anyone writing multiple-choice questions in law is to compose distractors that are plausible (especially if you read them fast enough) but will yield to careful analysis.

[3] In 1973, 20th Century Fox released *The Paper Chase*, which you may have seen. It is about the challenges encountered by first-year law students generally, set in the context of Harvard Law School. One of the first-year students upon whom the film focuses has an eidetic memory, but he gets into terrible trouble. He fails all of his mid-term examinations because, although he can remember *verbatim* every opinion that he has read, he cannot work with the material at all.

Mastering the law just is not about memorization. (Note that we said *"just is not* about memorization" rather than *"is not just* about memorization." There is a world of difference between the two.)

CHAPTER 2

The Method[1]

We thought we'd begin with a bit of heresy: stop looking for the "right" or ("best") answer by scanning all of the alternatives at once. Doing so prevents you from doing the necessary specific analysis of each alternative. Law does not lend itself to an intuitive approach. Going with your gut is at least as likely to lead you astray as it is to lead you in the most promising direction.

A Ten-Step Précis

1. Get a 3x5 (or 4x6) card.

2. If you possibly can, get a partner with whom to review.[2]

3. Cover the call of the question; do not read it yet.

4. Read the facts of the question slowly and carefully enough that you will not have constantly to refer back to them.

5. Slide the card down to uncover just the call of the question.

---

[1] Spoiler alert: the next chapter is not entitled "The Madness."
[2] Obviously you can follow our approach without a partner, but we think doing this method individually, at least at the beginning, is not nearly as effective as doing it with one other person.

6.   Get the issue about which the question asks firmly in mind, but *do not* hypothesize an answer.

7.   Slide the card down to uncover just Alternative A.

8.   Treat A (and every other alternative) as a true-false question. If it is entirely true, then it is a candidate answer. If any part of it is not true, then it is a reject.

9.   Explain specifically why A either is or is not a candidate answer.

10.   Slide the card down to expose Alternative B, and repeat steps 8 and 9 with it. Continue through the remaining alternatives.

Why This Way?

1.   The card is to prevent you from jumping ahead of where you should be with the problem. All of us have a tendency to go too fast, and on the MBE, that actually wastes time rather than conserving it. Deliberateness pays off handsomely. The card is your brake.

2.   It really helps to work with a partner, because your partner will not let you get away with a sloppy explanation.[3] You really will discover that doing this with a partner helps, because you will end up discussing the material in an organized way and cementing each other's understanding. Remember that you are engaged *studying* the subject, not *assessing* where you stand.

3.   Some people and some bar-review courses advise reading the call of the question first. That is certainly one rational way to approach questions, but we do not think it is the best way. Reading the call of the question first encourages you, as you then read the question itself, to begin to "see where this is going." Almost

---

[3]   Truth-in-advertising compels us to admit that Don was a repeat offender with sloppy explanations, not least because he had taught so much of the MBE material. Cyndy was a great partner; she did not (and still does not) let him get away with anything.

invariably, you will begin to hypothesize an answer—even before you have read the whole question. And here is the problem: having hypothesized an answer, you are then pre-disposed to jump at any alternative that even resembles your hypothesis, because it feels self-validating. As soon as you hypothesize an answer, to some extent you become emotionally invested in it. That makes dispassionate analysis even more difficult because of the psychological pressure that you have—quite unintentionally—created. And so we urge you simply to read the question first.

4.   Read the question slowly enough to retain the facts in your mind, so you don't waste lots of time backtracking. That doesn't mean you can never refer back to the question, but you need to be aware that reading the questions too rapidly, rather than saving time, ends up costing time because of the rereading it requires. Remember, as you are reading the facts of the question, that you don't even know yet what the question is! So don't guess at the issue, and don't try to answer the question in advance of analyzing each alternative. Just read the question as the beginning of a story. One of the characters will want to accomplish something, but there will be obstacles. The story is about confronting the obstacles and seeing whether it is possible to overcome them. That is what you should be thinking about. Every case, without exception, begins with a client with a problem.

5.   Now read the call of the question. Then you will know what the client's problem is. Do not look at any of the alternative answers yet. Do not (and this is difficult) hypothesize an answer to the question, for the reason we noted two paragraphs above.

6.   Note precisely what the question asks. Be aware that the MBE sometimes includes as an alternative the correct answer to some issue other than the one the question actually raises, and one is apt to be so excited at finding a fully true statement to overlook

that it is the answer to a question not asked. Do not hypothesize an answer.

7.   Once you know what the question is, slide the card down a bit more to uncover alternative A—no further.

8.   There are two possibilities for alternative A: either it is a candidate answer or it is not.

9.   If you think it is not a candidate, force yourself to verbalize precisely *why* you are rejecting it. Do not allow yourself the seductive luxury of simply thinking, "Well, this is obviously a crock." You may be correct; it may be a crock, but what is it that leads you to that characterization? Treat *every* alternative as a true/false question. If you think it is false, what makes it false?

10.   When you have finished alternative A, move to alternative B. Now it's your partner's turn to decide whether it is a candidate answer or, if not, what exactly disqualifies it. (This is also where you can get back at your partner for making you squirm.) Now you can continue to go through the remaining alternatives, one by one. Even if you think A is absolutely the correct answer, do not forgo doing the analysis for each other alternative. There are two reasons for this. First, one of the remaining alternatives may suggest to you something that you overlooked with respect to the problem. Second, and more important, is that we are trying to introduce to you a method of *studying for* the MBE, and the more alternatives you analyze, the more studying you are doing.

We think it is better *not* to look at all the alternatives at the beginning. When you do so, you are playing the alternatives off one against the other rather than analyzing each on its own merits. Treat each alternative as a true-false question standing alone. If you think it is at all false, identify precisely what makes it false. Does it depend on facts not in the question? Does it ignore facts that *are* in the question? Does it misstate the governing principle? Does it fail to take into account an exception to the usual rule? Does it state a rule of law that doesn't exist? Does it state a rule of law in absolute terms, using or implying words such as "always" and "never." If you think it is entirely true, then it is a candidate answer. But it is only a candidate; you cannot know that it is the best answer until you have analyzed all of the alternatives.

Continue with alternatives C and D this way, and do many, many more questions. You will discover that your speed increases and with it your confidence. By the time we got to the California Bar Examination, we had both practiced this method with so many hundreds of questions that we could do them rapidly enough to fit well within the time allowance for the examination.[4] (IMPORTANT NOTE: As far as we know, the bar examiners in every state tend to frown on working with a partner *during* the examination, but if you have diligently practiced in a rigorous manner, you will no longer need a partner. (You can always try visualizing whether your partner would accept the explanation you are thinking about.))

Caveat: Except for one type of MBE question, a multiple-choice alternative is *never* wrong "because another alternative is right." If that's what you are thinking, then you are not doing a complete job. Each alternative must stand or fall on its own merits. Think "true/false," not better/worse.

The exception: Some MBE questions ask what is the "best argument" or "worst argument" or "best available theory of recovery" or "most serious crime of which the defendant may be convicted." Then you must compare alternatives. In Criminal Law, that may mean that one or more lesser included offenses will appear as alternatives to the answer the examiners have designated as

---

[4]   In each session of the MBE, you have to complete 100 question in three hours. That is one minute and forty-eight seconds per question. If that does not sound like much time to you, set a timer (or have someone time it for you) and just sit for that amount of time. Don't look around; don't think about tonight's dinner; just sit. Most people begin to get antsy at about fifteen seconds.

correct. In best/worst questions (often appearing in Constitutional Law), that calls for knowing the courts' history of receptiveness or hostility to a particular line of argument. For example, it is usually easier to prevail on an equal-protection challenge than on a substantive-due-process challenge. Similarly, courts are often more receptive to an as-applied challenge than to an on-its-face challenge. These types of questions can be quite difficult; fortunately, there are never too many of them, but it is fair for the MBE to ask this type of question. You must know how to distinguish more promising arguments from less promising ones, and, when there are several theories of the case possible, which is the most likely to be persuasive to a court. That is sometimes murky. It is also a major part of our profession.

At this point, you may be wondering why in the world you should put in the considerable effort to master this procedure. The oversimplified answer (which you should, of course, reject) is that it works. We have taught this to hundreds of law students over the past thirty-five years. Only one was unable to master it, and that was because the student did not understand large amounts of the underlying material nearly well enough.[5] One student from a different school found her way to Don (we don't remember how), having failed the New York bar examination six times. She passed on the seventh because she nailed the MBE. That reflected a lot of hard work on her part, and it was hard work done the right way.[6]

Consider the benefits of doing what we suggest. First, for each question, you end up reviewing four principles in that area of law, not just one. Second, you are reviewing the substantive material in

---

[5]   You doubtless heard professors in your first-year courses caution you that there really are no "shortcuts" to mastery; you have to do the hard skull work. To be sure, there are lots of shortcuts, but none that will not impair your acquisition and honing of the critical analytical skills and judgment.

[6]   Don didn't do anything magical. The student knew the material well enough; she just did not know how properly to attack multiple-choice questions. She and Don did un   ls of questions together. She did all the work.

context, not in the abstract. It is much harder to remember the principles of any field of law in the abstract; it leads to oversimplification and sloppy analysis. Doing careful analysis for hundreds of questions (and four times that many alternatives) really cements the principles in your minds because you see how they work in what people laughingly call the "real world." We have also found, in working with hundreds of students who have felt themselves deficient in one or more subject areas, that they really know the material far better than they think they do. When they face fact patterns and questions, the legal principles come back to them, perhaps slowly at first, but more and more rapidly as they do more and more practice questions. If you have studied in a professional manner throughout school,[7] you *do* know the material; it's just a question of what it takes to pry that knowledge loose from your memory vaults.

We think your studying will be more effective and more rewarding if you work in this manner. Ours was. Many others have prevailed as well. We hope you will be successful in joining them. The MBE can be your strongest part of the examination if you will make it so. Start early, practice diligently, and watch your scores improve.[8] We wish you well.

---

[7] That does *not* mean studying every waking hour, or even close to it. It means spending a lot of time studying, but you need to continue your other activities as well, including exercise, sleeping, and incorporating some you-time in each day. This is even more important during your preparation for the bar examination.

[8] One student with whom we worked called us a mere two weeks later and said that his bar review course wanted to know what he had changed, because his scores on the course's practice examinations had shot up so dramatically. Now, it really wasn't because he had learned so much law in a fortnight; he had just found out how to get more effective access to what he already knew.

CHAPTER 3

Some MBE Patterns and an Important Caution

We will begin with the caution: as you are taking the MBE (or any other multiple-choice examination), never, *never*, **never**, **NEVER** leave any question blank.[1] That is because by the time you get to the end of the *next* question, you may have forgotten that you left one blank. If you were to skip Question 25, for example, by the time you finish reading, analyzing, and pondering Question 26 you may fill in your selected answer where the Question-25 answer should have gone (because it's the next available space, and you may not remember that you skipped 25). This has happened to students, and they often don't notice the error—until they get to Question 100 and start to fill in the answer in the next blank line on the answer sheet, which, unfortunately, is the line for Question 99. We characterize this as "slipping the grid," and, depending on where the slippage happened, it can be impossible to recover from it in time. This leads to a reaction most presentably summarized as, "Oops!!" but for which you might choose considerably different language indeed.

---

[1] Don't do it. Really. We're serious.

That is not to say that you may never want to come back to a question to give it more thought. There's nothing wrong with that, but instead of leaving it blank, fill in *something*, and make a tick mark next to the number of the question on your answer sheet so that you can find it quickly. There also may be questions that just blow you away; you look at them and think, "I have no clue!" Sometimes that happens. Decide before the examination what your "default" answer is. If you get one of those questions, don't waste time on it; it will only upset you. Fill in your default answer, make a tick mark in the margin, and come back to it later.[2] Remember that the MBE is 200 questions. No single question or small number of questions is ever going to make much difference unless you allow it to psychologically.

There are two MBE answer patterns to which you should be alert. Almost every MBE question asks you the outcome of a particular case or motion, and the answers then are in the pattern of, "Yes, because . . ., or "No, because . . . ." Your job is to evaluate the "because" statements to see which one of them resolves the issue. (1) Sometimes the "because" statement is absolutely true, but the result given ("yes" or "no") is the *opposite* of what would happen. (2) Sometimes the "because" statement is true, *and* the result is correct, but the "because" statement does not *cause* the result. Those are really tricky, because your mind is so excited to find a true statement juxtaposed with the correct outcome that you are apt to have a buzz-word or knee-jerk reaction and select that alternative. Neither the buzz-word nor the knee-jerk approach is notably successful on bar examinations (or any other examinations).

---

[2]   When Don was studying for the California bar, he had his materials spread out on the dining room table and took a break. When he got back, he saw the tiniest possible Post-It note in the middle of the page, on which his brother-in-law (a civil engineer) had written in nearly microscopic print, "The correct answer is almost always 'C.' " That became his default answer. You are welcome to use it; he is done with it.

Here is an example of that second phenomenon:

D, emerging from a local grocery store into the store's unfenced parking area, saw P, a teenager, placing leaflets on car windshields, including D's. D accosted P, grabbing P by the arm, and demanded that P return to D's car and remove the leaflet. P struggled, but was unable to break D's grip. D berated P for about a minute and then released P.

On these facts, is there false imprisonment?

    A.   No, because an outdoor parking lot is not a bounded area.

    B.   Yes, because D committed a battery.

    C.   No, because there was no substantial confinement.

    D.   Yes, because P was unable to break D's grip.

Let's consider the alternatives one by one.

    A.   True or false: an unfenced outdoor parking lot is not a bounded area. The "because" statement is true. But, did the parking lot restrict P's movement? Of course not. Did anything restrict P's movement? Well, yes; D's grip restricted P's movement to the bounded area of D's arm's length (since P was unable to break free). Therefore, "A" is not a candidate answer; the true statement about the parking lot does not prevent P from recovering.

    B.   This is a perfect example of what we are trying to illustrate here. True or false: D committed a battery. No question about it, right? P could include a battery count in the complaint and recover on it. *But* that is not what the question asks; it asks whether there has been false imprisonment. Well, there has been, but not *because* D committed a battery. Consider, for example, if D simply had punched P in the arm. That is a clearly a battery, but it is not false imprisonment. "B" is not a candidate answer; there is no causal relationship between the "because" statement and the result, even though each is *independently* true.

C.   True or false: there was no substantial confinement. Go back to one of your most reliable first-year answers in class: "it depends." Among other things, it depends on one's perspective. D would certainly characterize the confinement as insubstantial—only a minute. P, however, was struggling to break free. That alone is a hint that P thought the confinement was substantial; a minute can be a long time. But note what the "because" statement does here; it falsely implies that substantial confinement is an element of false imprisonment. "C" is not a candidate answer because it misstates the law by implication. The law of false imprisonment does not require "substantial confinement," whatever that may be.[3] *Any* confinement against the will of the victim suffices. More substantial (either because long lasting, dangerous, or unpleasant) confinements may lead to higher damage awards, but substantiality is not an element of the tort of false imprisonment.

So that leaves "D," but rather than choosing it because it is the only thing left, choose it because it includes a critical element of false imprisonment: restraint of movement. That sometimes occurs in a clearly bounded area—a room locked from the outside, for example—but it need not. The critical question is whether the victim was unable to leave, either because of physical restraint or because the victim could not attempt to leave without unacceptable risk.[4]

---

[3]   Just as beauty is a matter of individual perspective, so may substantial confinement be. High school detention passes unnoticed by students not in it. For those in detention (and the teacher), it seems very substantial.

[4]   For example, if A points a pistol at B and says to B, "If you take even one step, I will gun you down," that is false imprisonment. Restraint most often is, but need not be, physical.

Note you have just reviewed three factors related to false imprisonment and one involving battery—not too bad for a four-line question with one-line alternatives. You can make every practice question work for you in just this way.

Finally, it is occasionally the case that a question will have no candidate answer. Examiners do not do that intentionally, but they make mistakes just like the rest of us, so it happens. Don discovered one on the MBE in California in 1985.[5] The question dealt with standing, and the call of the question asked which of four groups was *the most likely* to have standing. Don had just published his second consecutive law review article on standing, and as he went through each alternative, he made a mental note of the Supreme Court's case holding that there was no standing. So he picked the answer he believed the questioner might have had in mind and moved on.[6] The important thing is not to get hung up on any single question.

Those "most likely" and "least likely" MBE questions are among the toughest, because they ask you to make predictions. You must evaluate the relative strengths of several possible arguments. So, as you go through the question, bear in mind how easy or difficult it is to dispose of each alternative. Usually some are less "crocks" than others. Fortunately, there are not a lot of such questions. Do the best you can, and move on. When you are practicing with your partner, spend some time discussing why one argument seems to

---

[5]   It was Question 177. Yes, he has that kind of mind. It's very sick.

[6]   That led to an interesting discussion with Cyndy on the way home. Don mentioned that there was no plausible answer to that question. Cyndy responded that the question only asked which group was *most likely* to have standing. Don's immediate reaction was that that was similar to asking which of four corpses is most likely to get up and walk away, depending on what it died from. It just isn't going to happen.

He does not know whether the answer he chose was the "correct" answer. California (at least then, perhaps still), only allowed review of the examination if the individual failed. That seemed too high a price to pay for curiosity.

you stronger or weaker than the others. That promotes deeper understanding of the principles.

The MBE has the reputation of making it easy to dispose of two alternatives and really difficult to choose between the remaining two. We found that using the method we recommend rarely results in that conundrum. For almost every question, there is a "right" answer or a "best" answer. You just need to take the time and have the discipline to ferret it out.

Now it is time for some practice. Step 1: get that 3x5 card. Step 2: Please remember that the goal is to teach you the technique of approaching multiple-choice questions that will improve your performance on the MBE, not to teach you the substance of the law. Obviously we will talk a lot about substance, but the important thing is how to approach and take apart multiple-choice questions in a logical, systematic way. The thinking process, much more than the answer, is what is important here.

WARNING: We are going to take you through lots of questions. We are also going to repeat the technique we suggest for each question and each alternative. It may get a bit tedious, but we hope it will also give you lots of drill in how to study for MBE questions and how to take each alternative apart for analysis. Our explanations will be far longer than yours need to be, and we won't use the various shorthand terms all of us develop to condense long-winded concepts into more compact form. After you have gotten used to approaching questions in an organized way, you will no longer need our extended treatment of them as illustrations. That's great; it's really what we are aiming for.[7] Keep in mind the process. It looks like this:

---

[7]   One part of our purpose is to help you speed yourself up when doing the analysis we suggest. How do you get faster? A very old joke has a tourist in New York City asking a passer-by how to get to Carnegie Hall. The answer? "Practice, practice, practice."

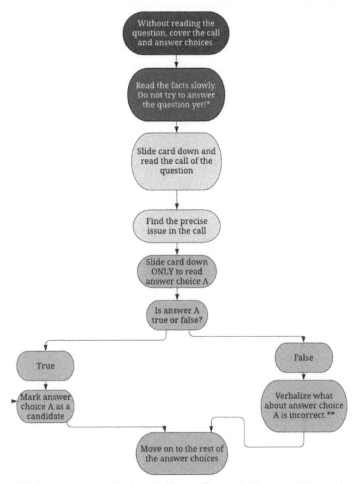

* You're not even supposed to have *read* the question yet. Don't guess at it; just read the facts with an open mind.

** Remember the things to look for in each alternative: (1) Does it state an absolute rule, omitting exceptions? (2) Does it assume facts not in the problem? (3) Does it state a non-existent rule of law? (4) Is *each* part of a compound statement true? (5) Is the "because" statement true, but the result the *opposite* of what would happen? (6) If the "because" statement is true, and the result is correct, does the "because statement actually *cause* the result?

CHAPTER 4

Technique Practice Questions

Torts

THE FOLLOWING FACTS APPLY TO QUESTIONS ## 1-8, WITH MODIFICATIONS AS INDICATED.

1. Defendant absolutely hated having drivers follow too closely. Every day Defendant drove to and from work on a major interstate highway, and every day Defendant got angrier about these "tailgaters." Finally, Defendant decided to teach them a lesson. A bit of an amateur mechanic, Defendant installed a device on Defendant's car that would simultaneously illuminate the brake lights and raise the rear while lowering the front of the car, as if it were stopping short, but without actually slowing it at all. Thus, Defendant hoped to get the results of a "brake-check" without actually subjecting either vehicle to increased danger of collision.

    The day after the installation, Defendant was driving on the interstate in the center of three lanes, fuming about the car behind, which seemed to be following at about a one-car-length distance despite the fact that both vehicles were going 65 miles per hour. Defendant activated the new device, which performed perfectly. Plaintiff, the driver behind Defendant, perceiving that Defendant's car was braking sharply, swerved to avoid the anticipated rear-end collision. Plaintiff's car ran off the highway and struck a large road sign, which collapsed on the car, doing extensive damage to the car and injuring Plaintiff severely.

IMPORTANT NOTE: If you have already begun analyzing in your mind, *stop*! You are going too fast. You don't even know yet what the question is. Except for the subsection's title, you don't even know whether this is Criminal Law or Torts. We have some perhaps disappointing news for you: the MBE does not label any question according to the subject with which it deals. Focus on carefully reading the facts and keeping them in your mind so you don't have to jump back and forth from each alternative to rereading the question. It may take you longer to read the question well enough to do that, but it will save much more time than it takes.

If Plaintiff sues Defendant for assault, the most likely result is that:

A.   Defendant will prevail because he intended no injury to Plaintiff.

Let's consider this alternative by itself. (You're not looking below this line, right? C'mon; indulge us for a while.) True or false: Defendant intended no injury to Plaintiff? On the facts given, it is at least arguable that Defendant intended no injury to Plaintiff (unless one counts scaring someone as injury). Do not even *think* about battery or intentional infliction of emotional harm. Perhaps it is emotional harm; perhaps not—more likely not—but the point here is not to get sidetracked. The question asks only about assault, and that is the only thing you should be analyzing.

What is *wrong* about this alternative, if anything? The unspoken legal premise underlying it is that there can be no assault without an intended injury. But is that so? Of course not! This is an alternative that by implication *misstates the law*. That is one of the things to look out for on the MBE.

What are the elements of tortious assault? Well, there are two: (1) the defendant must deliberately act to cause the plaintiff to apprehend an imminent battery, and (2) the defendant must either *intend* or be *substantially certain* that his conduct will cause apprehension of an imminent battery.

With respect to the first element, remember that under the law of torts, the soon-to-be plaintiff need not "fear" the imminent battery; the plaintiff need merely perceive that a battery is in the offing. Perhaps the plaintiff "lives for thrills" and is elated when something like this happens. Perhaps the plaintiff's self-view is that plaintiff is the second coming of daredevil Evel Knievel. That does not matter; the element of the tort is "apprehension" (meaning "perception") of an imminent battery, not "apprehension" in the sense of "fearing" an imminent battery.

On the facts, it certainly appears that Defendant had the requisite mental state; he was "teaching a lesson." And the defendant certainly acted in a way to produce the result. "Intended injury" is no part of the elements of assault.[1] So Alternative A is not a candidate answer.

B.   Plaintiff will prevail because Defendant is strictly liable for acting recklessly.

---

[1]   Since we are reviewing, remember that intended injury is not a necessary element of battery either, because the essence of battery is any unconsented-to touching. It may result in injury; it may simply result in offense. For purposes of establishing liability, that does not matter. For purposes of establishing damages, it may matter quite a lot.

True or false: Defendant is strictly liable for acting recklessly? Think about it for a moment. This is not a candidate answer either, but why not? The sentence is incoherent. There are several reasons. First, strict liability does not require any mental state—that's what characterizes it as *strict* liability.[2] So the implication that there is a state-of-mind component to strict liability is a *misstatement of law*. Defendant may end up being liable for driving recklessly, but not on a strict-liability theory.

Second, Defendant's conduct was beyond recklessness. Defendant did not elect to proceed in the face of a known risk that the reasonable prudent person would avoid; Defendant instead set out to create the appearance of a risk that a driver in a following car would perceive and react to, and that the reasonable prudent person would avoid creating. That was Defendant's plan. Third, assault is not a strict-liability offense, and the question asks only about assault, not about other theories of liability.

C.　Defendant will prevail if Plaintiff was following too closely.

True or false: plaintiff was following too closely? In most, if not all, states, following too closely means being so near the car in front as to be unable to stop without hitting it. In one way, "C" is an appealing answer, but it is a wrong answer. Plaintiff following too closely is almost certainly negligent, probably reckless. But the question asks only about assault, and neither negligence nor recklessness is a defense to an intentional tort. So this is not a candidate answer either. This is also a *misstatement of law by implication*, the implication being that Plaintiff's negligence is a defense to a claim of intentional tort.

---

[2]　So, for example, the statement, "Defendant is strictly liable even though Defendant acted with truly extraordinary care," is true, *provided* that Plaintiff's claim is for a strict-liability tort, such as carrying on some ultrahazardous activity.

D. Plaintiff will prevail because Plaintiff perceived an imminent collision with Defendant's car.

Well, yes; it's the only alternative left, but that doesn't necessarily make it the best answer. It is the correct answer to this question because it is the only alternative that speaks to the elements of the tort of assault. True or false: Plaintiff perceived an imminent collision with Defendant's car? That's pretty obvious, isn't it?

Note, by the way, that Plaintiff's perception need not be reasonable, although it certainly was on the facts given. Plaintiff may be skittish, but remember the principle that the intentional tortfeasor takes the victim "as he finds him."[3] That does not mean that the defendant is at the plaintiff's mercy; the intent requirement protects the defendant from potential claims by what the law calls "scaredy cats" and from potential false claims. In this case, of course, Defendant had the requisite intent. In the language of the criminal law, one might say Defendant was malicious.

2. On the facts of Question # 1, suppose that Plaintiff includes a count of battery in the complaint. On that count, the most likely result is that:

A. Plaintiff will prevail because Plaintiff reacted in response to Defendant's action, and Defendant's action proximately caused Plaintiff's injury.

True or false: Plaintiff reacted in response to Defendant's action, and Defendant's action proximately caused Plaintiff's injury? First, notice that this is a compound sentence with "and" joining the two clauses. That means both subparts must be true for

---

[3] So does the negligent tortfeasor, but with an important difference. To the extent that the case involves comparative negligence, then the plaintiff's actions in the perilous situation must have been reasonable. Excessive skittishness, for example, *may* diminish or prevent plaintiff's negligence recovery. It will not diminish plaintiff's recovery for an intentional tort.

the whole thing to be true. Did Plaintiff react in response to Defendant's action? Sure. Did Defendant's action proximately cause Plaintiff's injury? Of course.

This is a candidate answer. Defendant wanted to simulate an imminent collision and succeeded. Plaintiff's response was perfectly foreseeable: emergency maneuvers at high speed on roadways often cause drivers to lose control of their vehicles. "But Defendant did not intend any physical contact," you may be thinking. That's certainly true, but is that a requirement for battery?

Let's not go too fast here. Physical contact *is* an element of battery. What about intent? Defendant did not set out to cause unconsented-to touching, and it may not have been substantially certain to happen. (Defendant's plan was that there not be.) But assault is an intentional, trespassory, tort. Recall that among the Fab-5 intentional torts stemming from the common-law trespass *vi et armis*[4] writ (assault, battery, false imprisonment, trespass to chattel, and trespass to land), intent transfers from one to another. Defendant did intend an assault, and that suffices for the intent element of the battery claim. This is a same-victim/different-tort situation.

The important thing here is not to jump at conclusions. If you are going too fast, you are likely to think that since Defendant intended no collision, there can be no battery. But, as you see, that's not correct. Keep in mind that the fastest way to go through the examination successfully may be to slow down on each question, counterintuitive as that sounds.

---

[4]   "At common law, an action for damages resulting from an intentional injury to person or property, esp. if by violent means, trespass to the plaintiff's person, as in illegal assault, battery, wounding, or imprisonment, when not under color of legal process. . . ." BLACK'S LAW DICTIONARY 1542 (8th ed. 2004).

B.   Defendant will prevail because he intended no touching of Plaintiff, and Plaintiff's ending up in an accident was not a substantially certain result of Defendant's conduct.

True or false: Defendant intended no touching of Plaintiff, and Plaintiff's ending up in an accident was not a substantially certain result of Defendant's conduct? Once again, there is a compound statement that is conjunctive ("and") rather than disjunctive ("or"). Both parts need to be true for the statement as a whole to be true.

Is it true that Defendant intended no unconsented-to touching? The facts say so, and note that Defendant rigged the device so it would not actually slow Defendant's car; it would only appear to the driver behind that it was doing so.

Is it true that Plaintiff's ending up in an accident was not a substantially certain result of Defendant's conduct? This might be a bit of a closer call, but it is nonetheless correct. Defendant intended Plaintiff to brake sharply to avoid colliding with Defendant's apparently slowing vehicle. To be sure, Defendant created a significant risk that there might be a collision, but that is far less than a substantial certainty. If someone had been following Plaintiff too closely, that person would also have had to hit the brakes hard.[5] But substantial certainty? No; it was not substantially certain that someone would be following Plaintiff too closely,[6] nor was it substantially certain that Plaintiff would collide with Defendant—and Plaintiff did not.

This is not a candidate answer, although one may find it appealing. It tracks the alternative mental elements of battery. However, again there is an unspoken—and incorrect—implication. This alternative connotes that a successful claim for battery

---

[5]   Defendant, doubtless, would regard that as a double reward.

[6]   We live in California. Driving on a California freeway makes it a lot closer to substantially certain that someone will be following too closely at high speed.

requires one of the specific mental elements *for battery*. The last sentence sounds logical, if you read it fast enough. How else can one satisfy the mental element of battery? Remember at this point that having the required state of mind for any of the Fab-5 satisfies the required mental state of mind for any of the others—transferred intent.

The facts make clear that Defendant intended only to frighten Plaintiff to "teach him a lesson." *But,* we are in Intentional Tortsland, and transferred intent applies. Defendant unquestionably had the intent required for assault. Defendant fully intended Plaintiff to perceive an imminent collision. Remember the patterns in which transferred-intent liability may apply: (1) same victim, same tort, unintended consequence, (2) different victim, same tort, (3) same victim, different tort, (4) different victim, different tort. This is a case of same victim, different tort.[7]

C. Plaintiff will prevail because Defendant acted unreasonably.

True or false: Defendant acted unreasonably? If you think Defendant acted reasonably, then please let us know whenever you plan to drive so we can preemptively get off the roads. Yes, it is unreasonable by any definition to act in order to cause another

---

[7] Do yourself a favor. Stop reading now, and construct one hypothetical in each of these four patterns. Creating the hypotheticals will cement the patterns in your mind.

That sort of work pays off in many subjects. For example, you know from Civil Procedure that judicial jurisdiction comes in two flavors: subject-matter jurisdiction and personal jurisdiction. You also know that a court may have one without the other. To improve your understanding of the relationship between the two, construct four hypotheticals: (1) both subject-matter and personal jurisdiction exist, (2) neither subject-matter nor personal jurisdiction exists, (3) subject-matter jurisdiction exists, but personal jurisdiction does not, and (4) subject-matter jurisdiction does not exist, but personal jurisdiction does. Your hypotheticals need not be at all complicated. You can do them with two parties and very simple facts. At the end, you will understand the difference between the two flavors better than you may now. Don't just think about the possible patterns; *work with them*.

driver to perceive an imminent collision for the purpose of "teaching a lesson."[8]

This is not a candidate answer either. Unreasonableness is an element of negligence liability, but the question concerns an intentional tort. The "because" statement is accurate, but it does not *cause* Plaintiff to prevail in an intentional-tort action.

This alternative exemplifies one of the MBE answer patterns about which we warned you. *See supra* page 18 (2). It is true that plaintiff will prevail in the battery action, and it is true that Defendant acted unreasonably. It is, however, emphatically *not* true that Plaintiff will prevail in her battery action *because* Defendant acted unreasonably. That, at most, could result in negligence liability. And yet it is tempting, when one sees an alternative in which both the conclusion and the explanation are independently true, to have a knee-jerk reaction and select the alternative. That's how one loses points on the MBE. (There are other ways to lose points as well, but this is one of the stars.)

  D.   Defendant will prevail because Defendant did not slow Defendant's vehicle at all, and the two vehicles never came into contact.

True or false: Defendant did not slow Defendant's vehicle at all, and the two vehicles never came into contact? This is another compound, but nonetheless true, statement. Both parts are correct. So what remains is for you to decide whether the truth of that statement will cause Defendant to win the case.

This is not a candidate answer, even though the "because" statement is true. This is the other pattern we warned you about. *See supra* page 18 (1). There are many ways to cause a battery. If a

---

  [8]   Distinguish that from a situation in which a driver sounds the car's horn to warn another driver of an impending danger. That is a reasonable action. (Sounding one's horn to express frustration is not a reasonable action. (New York City drivers, take note.) And it may be dangerous, because it both expresses and invites road rage.)

defendant takes a swing at an intended victim, and the victim ducks to avoid the punch and strikes his head on an adjacent piece of furniture, the defendant has committed battery. In some sense, isn't that what Defendant did here? Plaintiff perceived (consistently with Defendant's intention) an imminent collision and took evasive action. Contact occurred as a result of Plaintiff's evasive action. The fact that Defendant did not intend contact is irrelevant, as is the fact that the contact occurred in a manner that the defendant may not have anticipated. This is a case of same victim, different tort, unintended consequence.

3.   Following the accident, Plaintiff was unable to leave the damaged vehicle for nearly ninety minutes; the damage to the car required use of the "Jaws of Life" to cut Plaintiff out of the wreckage. The accident trapped Plaintiff in the partially crushed vehicle in a very uncomfortable position. If Plaintiff includes a count of false imprisonment in the action against Defendant, will he prevail?

A.   Yes, because being trapped in a damaged vehicle is a foreseeable result of a collision.

True or false: being trapped in a damaged vehicle is a foreseeable result of a collision? Of course it is foreseeable; that's why someone invented the Jaws of Life. Does the truth of that statement mean that Plaintiff will recover?

This is not a candidate answer, even though the "because" statement is true. This answer would apply equally well to an accident resulting from negligence, yet if the defendant were only negligent, false imprisonment would not lie because the intent element would be missing. *See supra* page 18 (1). Any time you see "foreseeable" or "reasonable" or "unreasonable," you should be thinking about negligence; just don't become so fixated on it that you forget the call of the question. The question here asks about false imprisonment, not negligence, so the fact that Defendant might be liable on a negligence theory is irrelevant.

B.   No, because Defendant does not satisfy the intent requirement for false imprisonment.

True or false: Defendant does not satisfy the intent requirement for false imprisonment?

Before you can answer that, you obviously must know what the intent requirement is, and what leaps first to mind is that Defendant must intend to restrain Plaintiff's movement. Fair enough, but is that the only possible intent element? After all, an intent element of battery is the purpose of causing unconsented-to touching—but that is not the only intent element of battery; substantial certainty of causing unconsented-to touching also suffices. Are there any other intents that satisfy the mental element for the tort of false imprisonment?

This statement is not true because it *misstates the law of Torts* by implication, suggesting that there is no transferred-intent doctrine. But that's wrong, isn't it? The defendant had the intent required for assault. Among the "Fab Five" torts (assault, battery, false imprisonment, trespass to land, trespass to chattel) the intent to commit any one transfers to any of the others.

C.   Yes, because the doctrine of transferred intent is available.

True or false: the doctrine of transferred intent is available? It certainly is, provided that the "transferor" tort and the "transferee" tort are both members of the same club—the "Fab Five" torts (assault, battery, false imprisonment, trespass to land, trespass to chattel).

This is a candidate answer. Defendant's intent to assault (that is, to cause the victim to perceive an imminent collision), suffices as the intent for false imprisonment. This is a case of same victim, different tort.

>   D.   No, because the doctrine of transferred intent cannot apply to a tort different from the one the defendant intended.

True or false: the doctrine of transferred intent cannot apply to a tort different from the one the defendant intended? Certainly it can. A puncher may intend only to frighten the victim, but if there is contact between the puncher's fist and the victim's body, there is a battery.

This is not a candidate answer. Transferred intent applies in cases (1) where the harm defendant intended befalls an unintended victim, or (2) where the defendant intended to commit one of the trespassory torts but causes the kind of harm associated with another, whether the plaintiff was the intended victim or not. For example, if the defendant fires a weapon at A, intending to frighten but not to hit A, and the projectile strikes B instead, the defendant is liable to B for battery.

4.   In addition to the facts of Question # 1, suppose that Plaintiff's swerving vehicle cut across the right-hand lane of traffic, causing a car in that lane driven by Bystander to brake sharply to avoid colliding with Plaintiff's swerving vehicle. (In fact, it was not necessary for Bystander to have slammed on the brakes; Plaintiff's car would have passed in front of Bystander's vehicle, narrowly missing it, even if Bystander had not applied the brakes.) Passenger, in the back seat of Bystander's car, was not wearing a seatbelt and pitched forward because of the sudden braking, striking Passenger's face on the headrest of the front seat and suffering extensive dental damage. The state in which this incident occurred has a statute requiring each person in a car to use a seatbelt while the car is in motion and mandates civil penalties against

anyone not doing so. If Passenger asserts a negligence claim against Bystander, the most likely result on the issue of whether Bystander was negligent is that:

A. Bystander will prevail because the reasonable-prudent-person standard (RPP) does not apply in an emergency situation.

True or false: the reasonable-prudent-person standard (RPP) does not apply in an emergency situation? We are fairly sure that your Torts professor all but hollered (and may actually have hollered) at you about this. This statement is false—misstating the law—but it is one of the most common misperceptions among law students.

RPP applies in *all* situations. What changes is what the law expects from the RPP in an emergency. People who reasonably perceive themselves in emergency situations do not have time for the cool deliberation that we ordinarily expect from the RPP, and the law takes that into account, but it is clear that the RPP standard applies. So the proper question for emergency cases is whether, *in those circumstances*, the victim acted as the RPP would have.

So then the question is whether Bystander, perceiving Plaintiff's vehicle swerving at close range into Bystander's lane, did what the RPP would have done at that time. The threat from Plaintiff's vehicle was in the front; Bystander hit the brakes. Is that an RPP reaction? Most certainly. Note in hindsight that it may not have been the best thing to have done, but the RPP standard does not require that sort of careful weighing of alternatives in an emergency. The proper question is not whether Bystander's reaction was the best conceivable, but rather whether Bystander's reaction was rational.

So the "because" statement is false; the RPP standard *does* apply in emergencies. Accordingly, you immediately know that this alternative cannot be correct. Bystander *may* prevail ultimately, but not because of a false statement of law. And whether Bystander will ultimately prevail is not something that need concern you; no one asked that.

B.   Passenger will prevail because it was not actually necessary for Bystander to have stopped, so there was no emergency.

True or false: it was not actually necessary for Bystander to have stopped, so there was no emergency? You know the answer to that. The facts tell you that it was unnecessary, and there is no greater indicator of truth than inclusion of a statement in the fact pattern of a multiple-choice question. This is another point to be wary of going too fast. Fair enough; Bystander need not have braked (at least so sharply). But is that the correct measure for evaluating Bystander's action?

This is not a candidate answer, but again, the "because" statement is true. Hindsight is 20-20. The real issue is whether it was *reasonable* for Bystander to have perceived an imminent collision and to take the action Bystander did when Plaintiff's vehicle swerved sharply from an adjacent lane into Bystander's lane. After-the-fact analysis is not relevant. You may have had a similar experience (though we hope not arising from the same kind of malevolence as Defendant's here). Did you pause to consider the physics of whether (or how much) it was necessary to hit the brakes or take other evasive action? That takes quite a lot of calculation. (1) What was the other vehicle's forward speed? (2) How rapidly was the other vehicle coming toward your lane? (3) What was your forward speed? (4) At your speed, (a) did it seem necessary to brake at all, and (b) if so, how hard? (5) What is the slowing or stopping distance of your vehicle at that initial speed? (6) Would it have been possible for you to have swerved into an adjacent lane to avoid that risk without creating another, worse risk? (And all the subsidiary questions if there were other nearby vehicles.) C'mon! You act as an RPP would. How many of those observations and calculations did you make? (As your math teachers said, "show your work.")

C.   Bystander will prevail if Bystander reasonably perceived a danger of imminent collision and acted appropriately for that circumstance.

True or false? This is a candidate answer. *If* Bystander's perception of the need for immediate evasive action was reasonable, *then if* Bystander's reaction was reasonable *in the circumstances*, Bystander did nothing wrong, merely acting as the RPP would have, with unfortunate results.

D.   Passenger will prevail because Bystander was negligent *per se* in operating the vehicle while one of the occupants was not using a seatbelt.

True or false: Bystander was negligent *per se* in operating the vehicle while one of the occupants was not using a seatbelt? As Justice Scalia was wont to say, as a last resort one always could just read the words of the statute. Well, you don't have the statute's words here; you have a paraphrase. What does that paraphrase say? "The state in which this incident occurred has a statute requiring *each person* in a car to use a seatbelt while the car is in motion and mandates civil penalties against anyone not doing so." On whom does the seat-belt requirement fall? It is on "each person in a car." So does the statute cast liability on the driver if a passenger is not wearing a seat belt? Certainly not.

This alternative is not correct, though it may be appealing at first glance. It is only appealing if you have not read the question carefully enough. Negligence *per se* requires that the *defendant* have violated a safety statute and that the violation caused injury to the victim. But the statute casts the responsibility for wearing a seatbelt on the occupants individually, not on the driver as "captain" of the car. Passenger's failure to wear a seat belt is negligence *per se* on *Passenger*'s part, not on Bystander's. Now, one might argue that Bystander was nonetheless negligent for permitting Passenger to ride without a seatbelt. Perhaps Bystander was, but that does not respond to the call of this alternative, which asks about "negligence *per se*," not garden-variety negligence.

5.   On the facts as modified in Question # 4, does Bystander have a defense (other than Bystander's own lack of negligence, which Bystander certainly will argue) against Passenger's claim?

    A.   Yes, because both Defendant's and Plaintiff's actions exposed Bystander to the negligence claim, so Passenger's claim should run against them and not against Bystander.

True or false: both Defendant's and Plaintiff's actions exposed Bystander to the negligence claim, so Passenger's claim should run against them and not against Bystander? Let's take this one in pieces.

Is it true that the combined actions of Plaintiff and Defendant ended up exposing Bystander to the negligence claim? It certainly seems so; neither but-for nor proximate causation is difficult to establish in this situation.

Well, then, what about the second part of the statement, that "Passenger's claim should run against them and not against Bystander"? If Bystander was negligent, is it a defense to Passenger's action that there were other tortfeasors as well? In other words, is it a rule of the law of torts that the victim can only proceed against the earlier-involved tortfeasors but not against later-involved ones? If that "rule" doesn't sound at all familiar to you, good!

This is not a candidate answer. Here, most of the "because" statement is true, but not all of it.[9] Had Bystander acted unreasonably, Bystander would have been a joint tortfeasor. In addition, Bystander might have had a claim for contribution against the other tortfeasors, assertable either by cross-claim (if Passenger joined the other tortfeasors as defendants), impleader, or in a separate action. Nonetheless, the availability of that claim does not magically eliminate Bystander's own liability if Bystander behaved unreasonably. Bystander's ability to cut losses by filing other claims is not a defense to Passenger's negligence claim. All you really have to remember with respect to this alternative is that the majority rule is joint and several liability; a plaintiff can choose to sue one joint tortfeasor, some of the joint tortfeasors, or all of them.

B.   No, because Bystander assumed the risk that Passenger would be injured if Bystander got into an accident.

True or false: Bystander assumed the risk that Passenger would be injured if Bystander got into an accident? Note that "assuming the risk" is a term of legal art; it does not have its colloquial meaning.

Colloquially speaking, all of us assume multiple risks every day. We know, for example, that driving can be very hazardous, but we go out on the roads anyway. We know that if vehicle occupants wore helmets, their risk of serious head injuries in the event of a crash would be less. Still, other than racecar drivers, no one seems to take the step of wearing a helmet. Assumption-of-risk is now largely discredited; comparative negligence analysis has replaced it in all but a handful of United States jurisdictions. Even in its heyday,

---

[9]   To make the "because" statement true, it would have to read: "because both Defendant's and Plaintiff's actions exposed Bystander to the negligence claim, so Passenger's claim can run against them *and* against Bystander." It still would not be a candidate answer, however, because the result is incorrect. The fact that there are other tortfeasors whom Passenger can sue is not a defense for Bystander if Bystander was negligent.

assumption of risk did not merely mean doing something in the face of a risk that the RPP would recognize. The appropriate consideration is not whether the RPP would recognize the risk; it is whether the RPP would take steps to minimize or avoid the risk. You have been driving for years; how many passenger-car occupants have you seen wearing crash helmets?[10] The RPP takes risks as well. But, to *assume* a risk, one must act *without appropriate care and caution*, and one has to be *aware* of the risk. So even though we know that we expose ourselves to risk in driving, the law does not expect us to stay home all day or to walk everywhere—which itself comes with risk. There is no indication that Bystander knew that Passenger was not wearing a seatbelt. Passenger was in the back seat.

C.   Yes, because Passenger was negligent *per se*, reducing or eliminating any recovery by Passenger.

True or false: Passenger was negligent *per se*, reducing or eliminating any recovery by Passenger? Break it down.

Was Passenger negligent *per se*? The statute places the burden of compliance on each occupant of a vehicle. It is a safety statute. Passenger violated it. So we know the first part of the statement is true.

Then the question is whether that "reduc[es] or eliminate[s] any recovery by Passenger." What is the effect of a plaintiff's negligence in a negligence case brought by the plaintiff? The majority approach is to retain joint and several liability for the tortfeasors, to adjudicate negligence cases under some regime of comparative negligence, and to allow contribution among tortfeasors. (For purposes of this question, it does not matter which flavor of comparative negligence the state happens to use—pure,

---

[10]   This may do no more than to confirm your Torts professor's admonition that the RPP is a theoretical construct, not an actual individual.

49%, or 50%—that is merely a matter of how much potential recovery Passenger will forfeit),

Here it is important to remember precisely what the question asked: whether Bystander has an additional defense. It is also important to note what the question *does not* ask. It does not ask whether the additional defense will be successful; it merely inquires whether there is a plausible defense in addition to Bystander's lack of negligence.

Irrespective of your view of whether Bystander was or was not negligent, this is a candidate answer. If Bystander was not negligent, Passenger's recovery will fall to zero. If Bystander was negligent, the court will reduce Passenger's recovery proportionally to Passenger's degree of responsibility.

> D.   No, because Bystander was negligent *per se* in driving when Passenger was not wearing a seatbelt and could have avoided the harm to Passenger by simply refusing to drive until Passenger had buckled up.

This is not a candidate answer. (It is essentially a repeat from Alternative D in the preceding question.) It is clear that the statute imposed no burden on Bystander to ensure that *others* in the car were wearing seatbelts. Now, one might argue that Bystander was garden-variety negligent for not refusing to drive with an unsecured person in the vehicle, but that is not what this alternative posits.

Do not make the mistake of assuming that the availability of some additional safety precaution demands that the RPP take the precaution. The RPP is not required to take every possible precautionary measure; were it otherwise, there would be a thriving market in driver and passenger crash helmets. Remember Judge Learned Hand's "formula" from *Carroll Towing*: the RPP considers the risk of the harm occurring, the level of harm if it does occur, and the cost of taking precautions to prevent it. (This may eventually incline our society more seriously to consider requiring helmets.[11])

6.   On the facts as modified in Question # 4, does Passenger have a plausible claim against Defendant?

     A.   Yes, for battery, using the theory of transferred intent.

True or false: an unintended victim of an intentional tort can proceed against the tortfeasor? Well, transferred intent would be a fairly barren doctrine if the only situation it recognized were same victim, different tort.

This is a candidate answer. For the Fab 5 torts, the defendant's intent can "transfer" (which is simply a fancy way of saying "it counts") to unintended victims and unintended torts that are in the Fab-5 club. Just as Defendant may be liable to Plaintiff for battery, so also may Defendant be liable to Passenger for battery.

     B.   No, because Passenger was negligent *per se* for not wearing her seatbelt.

True or false: Passenger was negligent *per se* for not wearing her seatbelt? If you have read the question carefully, this gets a resounding "yes." Passenger certainly was negligent *per se*.

But let's not get so happy about seeing a true statement of law that our brains take a lunch break for the rest of the question. Does Passenger's negligence *per se* operate to defeat Passenger's intentional-tort claim against Defendant? There is also a resounding answer to this question, except that this time the answer is "no."

This alternative is not a candidate answer, though it is likely to be the incorrect distractor most selected by examinees who have

---

[11]   When Don began driving, no passenger cars even offered seat belts as an option. Now all states require them, and it is negligence *per se* not to wear them. The law does not consider the desire not to wrinkle one's clothes a sufficient reason for being unbelted. The day may come when the law won't consider "bad hair day" as sufficient reason for not wearing a helmet.

slipped into a knee-jerk or buzzword approach. It is true that Passenger is negligent *per se*, but it is equally true that the victim's negligence is *not* a defense to a claim sounding in intentional tort. Therefore, it might be a defense available to Bystander in Passenger's negligence action, but it is not a defense available to Defendant in Passenger's action for battery. This alternative rests on a *non-existent proposition of law*—that a plaintiff's negligence is a defense to a claim of intentional tort.

C.   Yes, for negligence, because Passenger's failure to wear a seatbelt provides a defense to Bystander but not to Defendant.

True or false: Passenger's failure to wear a seatbelt provides a defense to Bystander but not to Defendant *in a negligence action*? If you are thinking that Passenger's negligence is not a defense to an intentional tort, good for you, except that this alternative does not ask about an intentional tort; it asks about negligence. Was Passenger negligent *per se*? Certainly. Is that a defense in a negligence action against Defendant where Passenger's negligence contributed to the injuries? Why not?

This is one of those alternatives that sounds good if one reads it fast enough. The problem is that there is no basis for making the assumption that the statute is so limited. The purpose of the statute clearly is to require all vehicle occupants to take a particular safety precaution to reduce the risk of harm to them (and others) in the event of a crash. Whether the crash is the result of negligence by the driver of the passenger's vehicle, another driver, or a pedestrian who creates a hazardous road condition makes no difference. The crash may not be the result of negligence by anyone; accidents do happen. The purpose of the statute is to protect passengers from their own idiocy. Were Passenger to sue Defendant for negligence, Passenger's failure to wear a seatbelt *would* provide a defense—at least a partial defense—to Defendant.

D.   No, because Defendant took no action with respect to either Passenger or Bystander.

True or false: Defendant took no action with respect to either Passenger or Bystander? Defendant may not have intended to affect any driver on the road except Plaintiff when Defendant activated the device. Does that get Defendant off the hook with respect to Passenger? In other words, do intentional torts run only to intended victims?

This alternative gets back to transferred intent. The whole theory underlying transferred intent is that if someone commits one of the Fab-5 torts, liability arises with respect to anyone to whom the tort causes injury. Transferred intent says to the tortfeasor that foreseeability, quite relevant in negligence cases (see, e.g., Palsgraf[12]) is irrelevant with respect to intentionally acting in a tortious manner.

7.   On the facts as modified in Question # 4, assume (1) that Passenger sued all of the other actors and (2) that the state in which these incidents occurred follows a pure comparative negligence approach, retains joint and several liability and allows contribution among joint tortfeasors. The jury returns a special verdict against all three defendants, allocating responsibility as follows:

---

[12]   You do remember *Palsgraf*, do you not? Long Island Railroad, scales, platform, explosive package? That case was all about causation, specifically proximate causation. In this case, was Defendant's action so far removed from what happened to Passenger that it would be unjust to hold Defendant responsible?

(By the way, Cardozo, in addition to having the critical fourth vote in *Palsgraf*, also had the better of the argument. Judge Andrews asked the wrong question. The real issue was not whether there was a causal link between the Railroad's employees and Mrs. Palsgraf's injuries. The question Andrews should have asked, that Cardozo really did, was whether in the circumstances presented, the RPP would have appreciated and taken steps to avoid the risk of injury to Mrs. Palsgraf from the employees' attempt to keep the passenger from falling off the already moving train. Bear in mind that it was apparently an emergency situation; the passenger, in attempting to board the train, "seemed unsteady as if about to fall." What should the employees have done at that point? What was their duty? Should they simply have shouted, "Good luck, buddy"?)

Defendant: 45%,

Plaintiff: 30%,

Bystander: 5%, and

Passenger: 20%.

For each of the alternatives below that you think is incorrect, explain the misconception of tort law that the calculation represents. *The calculations themselves are all accurate.* If the jury assesses Passenger's damages at $10,000, the amount Passenger can recover from Bystander is:

[This is one of those questions that invites a knee-jerk answer, so it is important to slow down. Let's take this question apart.]

A. $10,000.

True or false: Passenger gets to recover $10,000 (never mind from whom the recovery would come at this point)? How could that be? Passenger's damages were $10,000, and the jury found Passenger's negligence was 20% responsible for the injuries.

This is not a candidate answer. Passenger is entitled to recover the percentage of Passenger's total loss for which Passenger is not personally responsible, so Passenger's recovery cannot be the full $10,000 because Passenger bears part of the responsibility for the harm. Passenger's responsibility comes off the top, as it were. (It is true, however, that Passenger can recover whatever damages Passenger is entitled to from any of the tortfeasors, irrespective of the individual tortfeasor's percentage of responsibility. That is the effect of the state retaining joint and several liability.)

B. 5% * $10,000 = $500.

True or false: Passenger recovers only $500 from Bystander? First of all, whence this $500 figure? That's Bystander's share of the negligence times Passenger's total damages, and that may make it appealing to you. But what kind of state are we in?

This is not a candidate answer either. It appeals to sloppy or too rapid reading of the question. The state in which this incident happened *retains* joint and several liability. That means that the victim can recover from any of the tortfeasors the total amount to which the victim is entitled, not merely the percentage of victim's loss that the jury attributed to a particular tortfeasor. The tortfeasors can fight it out among themselves if one ends up having to disburse in excess of the allocated share, but the possibility of contribution among joint tortfeasors has no effect on the victim's recovery. *If* the state had abandoned joint and several liability, *then* Passenger's recovery from Bystander could not exceed $500.[13]

C.   (5% * $10,000) * 80% = $400.

True or false: Passenger recovers $400 from Bystander? Look at what this calculation does. First, ignores the state having retained joint and several liability. Joint and several liability allows Passenger to collect all of Passenger's entitlement amount from any tortfeasor or combination of tortfeasors. What is Passenger's entitlement amount? Passenger suffered $10,000 in damages but was 20% responsible for that loss, and that 20% comes off the top of the potential recovery, reducing Passenger's total possible recovery from $10,000 to $8,000. What is Bystander's ultimate liability amount (after contribution)? Bystander's total responsibility is 5%. Passenger's total damages were $10,000. Bystander will ultimately be on the hook for $500. But then what happens in this alternative? One gets from $500 to $400 only by deducting Passenger's responsibility from Bystander's ultimate liability. But that is double-counting Passenger's negligence.

Consider it this way. Of the $10,000 harm that Passenger suffered, Defendant is ultimately responsible for $4,500. Plaintiff is

---

[13] Remember, in passing, that a state's decision to retain or discard joint and several liability shifts the risk of one or more tortfeasors' insolvency from the remaining tortfeasors to the victim.

responsible for $3,000. Bystander is responsible for $500. *Passenger* is responsible for $2,000. Those other figures ($4,500, $3,000, and $500) *already reflect* Passenger's 20% responsibility. To further reduce the other parties' shares by 20% (which is what this alternative does for Bystander's share) means that Passenger would ultimately recover not $8,000, the rightful share, but rather only $6,400, as if Passenger had been 36% responsible rather than only 20%. It is true that Passenger's responsibility share (20% * $10,000 = $2,000) comes off the top, but it only comes off the top once.

   D.   80% * $10,000 = $8,000.

This is the correct answer. Passenger's total loss is $10,000. Passenger's responsibility for the loss is 20%, so that comes off the top, leaving Passenger to recover $8,000 from the other actors, which, assuming no insolvency, they may end up dividing ratably. Passenger is still entitled to collect the full $8,000 from any of the tortfeasors, but if Passenger recovers from a single tortfeasor an amount greater than that tortfeasor's share, the overpaying tortfeasor can seek contribution from the remaining tortfeasors.

8.   On the facts as modified in Question # 7, if Passenger collects all that Passenger is entitled to from Bystander, and Plaintiff is insolvent (Plaintiff's share is P), the amount of contribution that Bystander can get from Defendant is:

   A. $4,500 + .90*P

This is the correct answer. Bystander has paid out the $8,000 to which Passenger was entitled. Of that $8,000, $4,500 is Defendant's share, and $500 is Bystander's share. The question really involves how to divide the "missing money"—Plaintiff's share (which is $3,000). For that, we look at the *relative* responsibility of the remaining tortfeasors—Defendant and Bystander. The jury found that Defendant's fault was nine times Bystander's fault (45% to 5%), so the "missing money" gets divided between them in a 9:1 ratio.

The "missing money" is $3,000, so Bystander is entitled to recover from Defendant $2,700 (.9 * $3,000) in addition to Defendant's own liability for $4,500. Note that the risk of insolvency of Plaintiff falls ratably on the remaining defendants. Had the state abandoned joint and several liability, Plaintiff could have recovered only $500 from Bystander and $4,500 from Defendant. The burden of the missing money would have fallen on Plaintiff.

B. $4,500 + .10*P

This calculation makes Bystander liable for a full 90% of the "missing money," not 10%. It is backwards.

C. $4,500 + $3,000

This calculation is incorrect because it casts the entire "missing money" burden onto Defendant, who should only have to bear 90% ($2,700) of it.

D.   Nothing, because the state adheres to joint and several liability, so Passenger was entitled to collect everything from Bystander.

This alternative is not a candidate. It certainly is true that Passenger was entitled to collect everything from Bystander. In the absence of contribution (*i.e.* under the old common-law approach), Bystander would have simply been out of luck, but the advent of contribution allows Bystander effectively to distribute the other tortfeasors' disbursements according to the jury's instructions. This alternative, therefore, is correct on the facts and correct about the state's law, but it arrives at the wrong conclusion. *See supra* page 18 (1).

* * *

Now take a step back, and see how much Torts review we have gotten in with just eight questions. The explanations for the inadequacy of the distractors touched on all the elements of assault (and battery), transferred intent, the eggshell-plaintiff rule, states of mind in torts generally, the distinction between intentional and unintentional torts with respect to defenses, emergencies, the reasonable prudent person, liability *versus* contribution, assumption of risk, comparative negligence *and* the importance of reading the call of the question carefully and tailoring your answer to it. To be sure, there was not complete review of each of those, but the explanations touch on them and bring them back to mind. That is not merely assessment; that's review. If you can discipline yourself to use sample questions to review in this way, you may surprise yourself how much better you can do. So at this point, let us repeat a caution: this method is slow at first—really slow. That is why it is necessary to begin practicing it early and to practice it often. If you do not practice with it before commencement, you probably will not have time to become comfortable using the technique before the bar examination. It may never be too late, but once you have begun your legal education, it's never soon enough.

Criminal Law and Procedure

1. While thoroughly intoxicated after a drinking binge following Parent's favorite team's victory, Parent drove Parent's sleeping children toward home well in excess of the speed limit. Parent crashed into the rear of a truck stalled in the middle of the road. One of the children died instantly in the crash. Trucker had failed to leave the truck's lights on or otherwise to give warning to approaching vehicles. Did Parent proximately cause the child's death?

    A. Yes, provided that the reasonable driver traveling at or under the speed limit would have been able to see the stalled truck and either steer safely around it or stop in time to avoid a collision.

True or false: if the reasonable driver would have been able to avoid the collision, then Parent is a proximate cause of the child's death?

This is a candidate answer. It posits that Parent's drunkenness made the difference between a fatal crash and no crash. It is, therefore a proximate cause of the death because it is related to the death closely enough to make society comfortable with imposing serious consequences.[14] Note that Trucker's negligence in taking no precautions to warn oncoming traffic is also a proximate cause. Many events can have multiple proximate causes just as all events have multiple causes-in-fact, going back to the Big Bang.

B.   No, because Parent is not responsible for Trucker's negligence.

True or false: Parent is not responsible for Trucker's negligence?

It is true that Parent is not responsible for Trucker's negligence, but is that all there is to it? Parent is responsible for Parent's own behavior. *See supra* page 18 (1). This alternative is a true statement of law joined with the wrong result. The alternative also assumes a non-existent rule of law—that there can be only one proximate cause of an event, but that is not so.[15] Note that the

---

[14] If you stop to think about it, that's all we mean by "proximate cause." Cause-in-fact ("but-for" causation) is an issue of physics, a question about whether some preceding act was a factor in causing a result. Cause-in-fact, standing alone, is never enough for liability, whether civil or criminal. All occurrences have multiple (really innumerable) causes-in-fact. For example, the fact that Parent's parents felt frisky one evening (or morning or afternoon) is a cause-in-fact of the crash. We trust no one would think it appropriate to fasten liability on them. Proximate causation is not a matter of physics; it is a matter of policy—whether society thinks it is *fair* (or appropriate) to blame someone far back in the causal chain for the results. More simply, it is the question of how far back is too far back, and the answers, as you know, can be complex and the arguments spirited.

[15] Here's a simple demonstration. Two cars are approaching an intersection from opposite directions. Neither is driving as the RPP would. As they enter the intersection, their vehicles simultaneously collide with a vehicle proceeding across the intersection at right angles to them, that vehicle's driver having driven entirely reasonably. If you think there can be only one proximate cause, which vehicle is it?

question does not ask what crime Parent may have committed, so you need not get hung up on whether it might be involuntary manslaughter, negligent homicide or something else. The question asks only about causation.

C.   Yes, because the law imputes Trucker's negligence to Parent because of Parent's failure to exercise due care.

True or false: the law imputes Trucker's negligence to Parent because of Parent's failure to exercise due care?

What is necessary to impute one actor's negligence to another actor? Imputed negligence requires some legally recognized connection between the parties, such as principal/agent or employer/employee. There is no relationship between Parent and Trucker, so there is no basis for imputing Trucker's negligence to Parent. Parent is liable for Parent's own conduct, not for Trucker's. This is not a candidate answer because it states a non-existent principle of law: that one's own negligence allows imputing of someone else's negligence.

D.   No, because negligence will not support a finding of proximate causation.

True or false: negligence will not support a finding of proximate causation?

If this statement were true, could the crimes of negligent homicide or involuntary manslaughter even exist? This is not a candidate answer because it is absolute. You should *always* be suspicious of absolute statements . . . except for this sentence.

As in Torts, negligence certainly can be proximate causation.[16] The standards for what constitutes negligence differ between the two subjects, but the question does not ask about that. Many states

---

[16] Your Torts course would have been a lot shorter if negligence could not provide proximate causation—*and*, you would not have had to read and understand *Palsgraf*!

recognize negligent homicide (usually called involuntary manslaughter).

2.   X, an employee of the United States Postal Service, learns that Y (whom X has never met) plans to break into the local post office to steal valuable first-day covers (which are of utterly no use to anyone other than stamp collectors). X harbors a grudge against the Postal Service stemming from what X perceives as its indifference to its employees. Hoping to cause the Postal Service embarrassment, X disables the alarm system before leaving work at the end of the day. Y arrives that evening, enters the building undetected, and makes off with first-day covers and assorted valuable office equipment. Brilliant detective work leads to the FBI arresting X. If the grand jury indicts X for conspiracy to commit theft, the court should find him:

A.   Not guilty, because X did not know that Y would steal office equipment and therefore had no *mens rea* to support a conviction.

True or false: X did not know that Y would steal office equipment and therefore had no *mens rea* to support the conviction?

Once again, there is a compound statement, so you need to break it apart and test its components individually. It is true that X did not know that Y would steal office equipment.

Then you should be asking yourself whether X had the *mens rea* to support a conviction *for conspiracy*. This is where you need to be careful. This is not a candidate answer simply because X acted to facilitate Y's theft. That makes X an accomplice, not a co-conspirator. There is no conspiracy because there was no agreement. (The fact that Y also stole office equipment is of no significance because X certainly had the *mens rea* for the stamp thefts, and it certainly is foreseeable that Y would not limit the theft to stamps.) This alternative implies a *misstatement of law*, that conspirators' liability extends only to the specific offense to which they all agreed, but as you know, conspiracy liability is broader than that. This alternative also invites you to answer a question that is not present in this problem: whether X is subject to any criminal liability or whether X is an accomplice. All this question asks about is conspiracy.

B.   Guilty, because X is liable for crimes that are a foreseeable part of the conspiracy venture, and it was foreseeable that Y might not limit the theft to postage.

True or false: X is liable for crimes that are a foreseeable part of the conspiracy venture, and it was foreseeable that Y might not limit the theft to postage?

Note what this alternative does; it *assumes* that there was a conspiracy venture, but nothing in the fact pattern supports that assumption. There is no agreement between X and Y. If the alternative said, "A *co-conspirator* is liable for crimes that are a foreseeable part of the conspiracy venture, and it was foreseeable that Y might not limit the theft to postage," then the statement would be true, **but** this formulation also assumes that a conspiracy exists.

So this is not a candidate answer. The "because" statement is true, *provided that* there *is* a conspiracy venture. It refers to an instance of the *Pinkerton* rule, which holds all conspirators responsible for foreseeable but not specifically agreed upon crimes committed in the course of the committing the target crime.

C.   Not guilty, because Y was unaware of X's assistance.

True or false: Y was unaware of X's assistance? Well, the facts tell you that the two have never met, and there is no indication of any communication between the two. So the statement is true. Then the question is where that leads us.

This is a candidate answer, although that may seem counterintuitive to you. It is an accurate statement of a critical fact in the problem. The essence of conspiracy is the *agreement* to commit a crime. There was no agreement here. Now, it is true that not all of the actors in a extensive conspiracy have to know each other or even have to know what other actors are doing. That's fine, but when there are only two actors, they *must* know each other. How else would they be able to make the agreement that is a fundamental part of the prosecution's case-in-chief on a conspiracy charge. Does this mean that X has committed no crime? Certainly not. X, though not a *co-conspirator* of Y, is most certainly an *accomplice* to Y's thefts. Complicity liability does not require any agreement between or among the perpetrators. X had the intent required for the crimes of larceny and trespass to land, and Y committed those offenses with X's aid, whether Y was aware of X's aid or not.

D.   Guilty, because it is not necessary for Y to be aware of X's assistance as long as X acted with the requisite *mens rea*.

True or false: it is not necessary for Y to have been aware of X's assistance as long as X acted with the requisite *mens rea*? In the context of this question, the statement is false.

This is, perhaps, an attractive possibility, but it is wrong. It *misstates the law* by implication, suggesting that agreement is unnecessary to a conspiracy. (What it really does is to state a rule of complicity law, and so it sounds attractive because for that area of criminal law, it is a correct statement. But, once again, the question asks about conspiracy, not complicity.) To be sure, X is liable for the theft as an *accomplice*, because complicity liability does not require that the primary actor know of the accomplice's assistance. A conspiracy conviction, though, is not possible without an agreement.

3. A, angry at his boss B for refusing to increase A's salary, decided to break into B's house. A intended to take B's diary (a booklet of no intrinsic value but of sentimental value to B), copy it and publish it on the internet, returning the diary to its original spot in B's house. When B was out of town, A entered the house by using the key B had given A to use in emergencies. No one was home. A located the diary and took it. The diary fell unnoticed[17] from A's his pocket and never left B's property.

    The state arrested A and charged A with burglary and larceny. If there is no dispute on the facts, is A guilty of burglary?

    A.   No, because A did not break into the house.

    True or false: A did not break into the house? False, right?

    This is not a candidate answer. The "because" statement may sound true. What makes it wrong is the implication (from the colloquial meaning of "break") that some sort of destructive force is an element of burglary. But as you know, the same word may mean one thing (or multiple things) colloquially and something quite different legally.[18] Common-law burglary did not require forcible entry such as breaking a window or battering down a door. The slightest force, such as pushing open a door that had been left ajar, sufficed. A's opening the door with the key satisfied the breaking-and-entering element of burglary.

---

[17] This leads to at least a reasonable suspicion that A was no better at being a thief than at being an employee.

[18] Take, for example, "conversion." Colloquially it may mean abandoning one religion and adhering instead to another. It may also mean changing the function of a room—converting it from a library to a rec room. It may mean trying for an extra point or two after scoring a touchdown. Those are all legitimate colloquial understandings of "conversion." THE RANDOM HOUSE DICTIONARY OF THE ENGLISH LANGUAGE lists well over ten meanings for "conversion that are *not* legal terms. Legally conversion has one of two meanings, as you can see in BLACK'S LAW DICTIONARY. For purposes of torts or criminal law, conversion means, roughly treating as one's own property that to which someone else has a superior possessory claim.

B.   Yes, because A entered in a non-emergency situation to steal the diary.

True or false: A entered in a non-emergency situation to steal the diary? False!

It is not a candidate answer for two reasons. First, A did not intend to *steal* the diary. A's intent was to return the diary, thus not satisfying the common-law requirement of intending to deprive the rightful possessor permanently. (This is why joyriding—taking someone's car to ride around in but intending to return it to the owner afterward—required a statute to criminalize it. At common law, the intent to return negated larceny.) Second, common-law burglary (as opposed, for example, to burglary under Model Penal Code § 221.1) required that the intruder intend to commit a *felony*. Taking a diary of no intrinsic value is not a felony.

C.   No, because A intended to take only the diary.

True or false: A intended to take only the diary?

Once again, the "because" statement is true, but this time it *does* negate an element of burglary: the intent to commit a felony. Therefore, this is a candidate answer.

D.   Yes, because A intended to use the diary to cause B great personal embarrassment, which might then have resulted in harm to B's business.

True or false: A intended to use the diary to cause B great personal embarrassment, which might then have resulted in harm to B's business?

This is a true statement of A's intent, and yes, it might have resulted in economic harm to B. The goal was to borrow the diary. Even if A had intended to steal the diary, the law does not grade larceny based on its ripple effects; the only relevant inquiry to determine whether there is grand or petit larceny is how much the purloined property was worth. A's intent to embarrass B with possible resultant harm to B's business, while perhaps reprehensible (that depends on who B is), is not a felony. This is not, therefore, a candidate answer.

4. On the same facts as in Question 3, if there still is no dispute on the facts, is A guilty of larceny?

    A. No, because A was unsuccessful in his attempt to make off with the diary.

True or false: A was unsuccessful in his attempt to make off with the diary? Well, it depends how you look at it. A certainly was unsuccessful in accomplishing the harm that A hoped to cause B. Think like a lawyer, though. The charge is larceny. What are the elements of larceny? If A raises as a defense the argument of A's incompetence,[19] to which element is A directing that defense?

While perhaps tempting, this is not a candidate answer. Look at what this alternative implies: that larceny requires some sort of clean getaway with the loot. But that is not a correct statement of law; there never was such a legal rule.

This alternative deals with the *actus-reus* element of larceny known as asportation. Asportation does not require a clean getaway. The slightest movement of the object the thief intends to steal suffices. A's picking up the diary satisfies the asportation requirement. (The intent requirement, obviously, remains.) If, when A picked up the diary, A intended never to return it, and later (even an instant later) had a change of mind and replaced the diary in its original position, there would still have been a larceny.

---

[19] Incompetence often comes up as a defense. Some consider attempt offenses as crimes for incompetent people. Don once persuaded a federal judge in a bench trial to acquit the defendant because of the defendant's incompetence to imagine a plan of action that would have satisfied the *mens rea* requirement of the statute. (In announcing the decision, the judge declared, "This man is a nincompoop." The defendant did not appear to understand.)

(Granted, there might be problems of detection and proof, but the question does not ask about that.)

B.   Yes, because A took possession of the diary.

True or false: A took possession of the diary? That certainly is true, is it not? A exercised dominion and control over the diary, albeit for a short time only.

At first glance, this alternative might appear to be a candidate answer. It certainly meets the objection to the first alternative. A's possession was temporary, to be sure, but A did exercise dominion and control over the book. But "first glance" is not a good strategy for the MBE. When confronting an MBE criminal-law question, you need to discipline yourself to focus on *all* of the elements of the offense. This alternative satisfies four of the elements of larceny. It does not satisfy the fifth—intent permanently to deprive the possessor of the property. A's plan was to return the diary. So this cannot be a candidate answer.

C.   No, because A intended to return the diary.

True or false: A intended to return the diary? Well, that's what the facts say, right?

This is a candidate answer. A's intent to return the diary negates an element of larceny. The intent element demands that the would-be thief intend to deprive the possessor of the item *permanently*. That intent is lacking here. (This is why joyriding—taking someone's car to ride around in but intending to return it to the owner afterward—required a statute to criminalize it. At common law, the intent to return negated larceny.)

D.   Yes, because A performed the last proximate act in commission of a theft.

True or false: A performed the last proximate act in commission of a theft?

True, with a huge "but." This alternative invites the buzz-word approach. "Last proximate act" sounds so familiar. And so it should; it is one of the requirements at common law for an attempt. But the charge against A is not attempted larceny, but rather the completed crime. In fact, since we are reviewing, there is no attempted larceny either. The intent requirement for attempt is the same as for the completed crime. A's intent to return the diary prevents conviction of the attempt as well. Had A not intended to return the diary, all the other facts being the same, A would be guilty of attempted larceny (as a lesser included offense) (but of course would not be subject to conviction for both the attempt and the completed larceny).

5. Alpha, Beta, Gamma, and Delta decided to rob a bank and planned the robbery as carefully as they could to avoid injury to anyone. Alpha, Beta, and Gamma were to pull off the robbery; Delta's job was to drive the getaway car. The first three entered the bank, armed and masked, and at gunpoint forced the tellers to give up the money in their drawers. To emphasize the seriousness of the robbers' purpose, Alpha fired several shots into the ceiling just before leaving, warning everyone in the bank not to move for five minutes. Alpha, Beta, and Gamma left and got into their car. Delta drove away very carefully to avoid attracting attention. Ten miles from the bank, on a remote back road, Delta saw Delta's Enemy walking down the road with Enemy's back to the car. Delta accelerated sharply, swerved, and hit Enemy, causing Enemy's death. Delta then returned to driving sedately down the road as if nothing had happened. Two months later, the police arrested the four perpetrators. The state has charged them with conspiracy, bank robbery, and murder.

The state tried Alpha, Beta, and Gamma together. If the jury accepts all of the facts recited, should it convict the three defendants of murder?

A.   Yes, because the conspirators had not reached a place of temporary safety when the killing occurred, so the underlying felony was still in progress.

True or false: the conspirators had not reached a place of temporary safety when the killing occurred, so the underlying felony was still in progress?

This alternative invites you to misunderstand the time element of felony murder. Killings in the course of committing the predicate crime qualify for felony murder. The question is how long a crime goes on (or when is it over). The standard is that the perpetrators have reached a place of temporary safety. That does not require that the felons stop and establish a domicile; it requires only that they are away from the scene and that there is no pursuit. Nothing in the facts indicates that there was any pursuit[20] and Delta was not driving as if there were any pursuit. They had reached a place of temporary safety.

B.   No, because they had taken great precautions to ensure that there would be no injuries resulting from the robbery.

True or false: they had taken great precautions to ensure that there would be no injuries resulting from the robbery? That's easy, right? The facts say they had. Then you need to ask yourself whether taking precautions in the planning and execution of the predicate felony negates any element of felony-murder.

---

[20]   Do not assume facts not in the question. You may expect that there certainly would be pursuit after such an incident. We may even hope that there would be. But the question does not say that there was any, so don't invent some.

This is not a candidate answer, even though the statement in the alternative is true. *See supra* page 18 (1). Under the felony-murder rule, the precautions the defendants take to avoid injury are irrelevant. The whole point of the felony-murder rule is to permit murder convictions when the intent to kill, ordinarily required for murder, is lacking. The intent to commit the underlying predicate felony suffices for felony-murder. (This is the criminal law's version of transferred intent.)

C.   Yes, because they were co-conspirators of Delta, and all conspirators are criminally responsible for crimes committed by any of them until the conspiracy's target crime is complete.

True or false: they were co-conspirators of Delta, and all conspirators are criminally responsible for crimes committed by any of them until the conspiracy's target crime is complete? This is a compound conjunctive statement, so you must evaluate each part of it individually. Were the other three actors co-conspirators of Delta? Certainly. Now, is the second part of the alternative true?

This is not a candidate, because it is a considerable overstatement of conspiracy liability. Co-conspirators are liable for the target crime of the conspiracy and for all other crimes in the course of committing the target crime that are foreseeable. They are not responsible for any unrelated crime that one of the co-conspirators decides to commit. The conspiracy had ended by the time Delta acted, because the conspirators had completed the target crime and had reached a place of temporary safety. Delta wasn't acting in furtherance of the conspiracy; Delta was settling a private grievance.

D.   No, because neither the conspiracy nor the bank robbery was a proximate cause of the killing.

True or false: neither the conspiracy nor the bank robbery was a proximate cause of the killing?

This is the best answer. The conspiracy and the bank robbery are causes-in-fact of the killing because they are in the chain of events that led to the killing. But then, so are the births of each of the conspirators, their parents having fallen in love, etc. Proximate causation (in both Torts and Criminal Law) is a matter of policy, not physics or cause-and-effect. The question the doctrine of proximate causation asks is whether a defendant's behavior was closely enough related to what happened to make society comfortable with visiting the consequences of the result on the defendant. With respect to everyone other than Delta, there is no doubt that they are guilty of conspiracy and bank robbery, but should we be comfortable with sticking them with liability for Delta's deciding to settle a private grievance?[21]

Constitutional Law

THE FOLLOWING FACT PATTERN APPLIES TO QUESTIONS ## 1, 2

A town code[22] provides in part that house owners may display only one real-estate for-sale sign per lot and further states:

Content of real estate signs

The sign content may contain the words "for sale" or "for lease," symbols, logos, QR codes (matrix bar codes), realty company name, realty agent's name, phone number, and web address. No other content is permitted, and no more than three colors are permitted.

---

[21]   This would be a much closer case if, during the robbery, Delta had recognized a passer-by as Delta's "private" enemy and had killed the passer-by as Delta accelerated away from the bank. But that is a problem largely of proof, and the question is not about that.

[22]   This is a real ordinance that was in effect in the town in which we used to live.

Removal of real estate signs by Building Inspector

(1)   The Building Inspector may remove any real estate sign that does not comply with this ordinance.

(2)   Such sign so removed shall be returned to the sign's owner upon the payment of a civil penalty for such violation in the amount of $75.00.

1.   Owner has a house to sell. Owner has retained a real estate company to assist in the sale. In addition to the information the ordinance permits, Owner includes on the sign the square footage of the house. If the town charges Owner with violating the ordinance, what is Owner's best argument against the ordinance's constitutionality?

[Note first that this is a best-argument question, and for those sorts of questions, the true-false approach does not work well. There may be more than one argument that is plausible; what the question asks you to do is to evaluate which has the greatest chance of success.]

A.   The code violates substantive due process.

This is not a candidate answer. The Supreme Court has always disfavored substantive-due-process arguments. The Court has recognized a few such rights but has limited them to rights it deems fundamental. There is no substantive-due-process right, when selling a house, to include the house's square footage on a sign advertising the sale. Substantive due process is always an uphill argument. Note that the First Amendment's Free-Speech clause is not part of substantive due process. The latter encompasses only rights that the Constitution does not enumerate.

B.   The code violates the First Amendment.

This is a candidate answer. but do not go too fast. Not every law that regulates or prohibits speech violates the First Amendment.

The for-sale sign is commercial speech, and the town may therefore regulate it in some, but not all, ways. The town can impose reasonable time, place, and manner regulations, and it can regulate misleading commercial speech.

Here the code is not a time-place-manner regulation, and it attempts to control dissemination of *accurate* information. The code dictates what information can go on a for-sale sign and proscribes any other information, such as Owner's notation of the house's square footage. (Note that, as the code reads, not even Owner's name can appear on the sign, even (apparently) if Owner is selling without using a broker.) Content-based restrictions are permissible only if they exist in support of a compelling state interest and are drawn in the narrowest manner possible to achieve the state's objective. It is difficult even to think up a state interest in forbidding signs from noting the square footage of the house; there certainly seems to be no *compelling* interest in suppressing that information.[23]

C.   The code interferes impermissibly with interstate commerce.

This is not a candidate. Not every local action that affects interstate commerce in any way is impermissible,[24] but the way this alternative reads may suggest the contrary to you. That is an absolute view of the Commerce Clause's scope, and as you know, absolutes in the law are hard to come by. Although one can

---

[23] It is difficult, but not impossible. The town may argue that the more information that appears on a sign by the street, the more drivers will look at the sign more closely (and for longer), thus distracting them from their driving duties and increasing the risk of an accident. On the other hand, because the ordinance specifies what is permissible, one might argue that it is not drawn in the narrowest possible manner to achieve the government's objective. For example, the government might specify how many lines or words a sign could contain, how large or small the print might be, and perhaps even something as vague as how distracting a sign could be. There is no apparent government interest in banning inclusion of a single piece of accurate information.

[24] Wickard v. Fillburn, 317 U.S. 111 (1942), (the back-yard-wheat case) to the contrary notwithstanding.

hypothesize a causal connection between sale of a private house and interstate commerce, it is not easy. Even taken in the aggregate, the town's code can only incidentally affect interstate commerce, and incidental effects are permissible.

    D.   The code is void for vagueness.

This is incorrect. Whatever the constitutional infirmities of the code, vagueness is not one of them. Laws that proceed by enumeration of either permitted or forbidden conduct are rarely vague. That is all the more true here, because there is no need for interpretation at all.

2.   Suppose Building Inspector seized Owner's sign and refuses to return it to Owner until Owner pays the civil penalty. If Owner brings a federal action against the Town and the Building Inspector seeking a declaratory judgment that the seizure-and-return part of the code is unconstitutional and an injunction compelling Building Inspector to return the sign, which of the following is the most likely result?

    A.   The defendants will prevail because the code is clear and unambiguous.

This cannot be a candidate answer. Look at the inference that this alternative suggests: any law that is clear and unambiguous is immune from constitutional challenge. That is a pretty gross misstatement, don't you think? The laws mandating school segregation were clear and unambiguous, but that did not save them from successful challenge in *Brown v. Board of Education* (1954).

The code certainly is not void for vagueness, but there are two other problems, one procedural and one substantive. Procedurally, the law disfavors seizure of property without a pre-seizure hearing unless emergent circumstances require it, and even then, the law requires a post-deprivation hearing. Here there are neither emergent circumstances nor a post-deprivation hearing. The code holds the sign for ransom. That is constitutionally impermissible. On the substantive side, the code is constitutionally defective because it impermissibly regulates protected speech.

> B.   Owner will prevail because the First Amendment prohibits the town from regulating the content of Owner's speech.

Not so fast! You should be suspicious of any alternative that states an absolute. The absolute here is that the government can *never* regulate the content of speech. You know that's not true. This is not a candidate answer.

This is commercial speech, and therefore is subject to some regulation. Its primary purpose is to promote a business transaction. But, assuming the listed square footage is accurate, there is nothing misleading about it. And what is the state's compelling interest in suppressing such limited, accurate information about a product advertised for sale? And, even if there is a compelling interest, has the state used essentially the narrowest possible way of achieving its objective so as to avoid unnecessary intrusion on Owner's First-Amendment rights? The other possible area of speech regulation involves time, place, and manner, but this code addresses none of those things.

> C.   The defendants will prevail because Owner violated the code.

We hope no one thinks this is a candidate answer. If it were true, no ordinance would ever be subject to constitutional attack. In many—almost all—constitutional challenges to laws, there is no serious question about whether the person subject to the law has acted or proposes to act in violation of its terms. (The overbreadth cases are exceptions.)

> D.   Owner will prevail on Fourteenth-Amendment grounds of procedural due process.

This is the best available answer. The town has provided no adjudicative process at all, simply seizing and holding private property until payment of a fine—holding it for ransom. There is no possibility of challenging the ordinance at any point. The seizure is a taking of property within the meaning of the Fourteenth Amendment, and that requires due process, either pre- or post-deprivation.

* * *

3. To conserve dwindling fossil fuel supplies and to limit air pollution, Congress enacts a statute denying federal highway funding to any state with a maximum speed limit more than fifty miles per hour. Is the legislation constitutional?

   A. Yes, because Congress has power to do that from both the Taxing-and-Spending Clause and from the Commerce Clause.

True or false: Congress has power to make eligibility for federal highway funding conditional from both the Taxing-and-Spending Clause and from the Commerce Clause?

This is a candidate answer. *South Dakota v. Dole*, 483 U.S. 203 (1987), upheld Congress's entitlement to deny highway funding to any state in which the drinking age was less than 21. There was a similar challenge to a federal statute prescribing no more than a fifty-five mph limit, and the Ninth Circuit ruled against the challengers. (The Supreme Court denied certiorari.) Congress can condition expending federal money on any basis that is not unconstitutional, and there is no constitutional right to drive a vehicle in excess of fifty miles per hour.[25]

---

[25] For apostles of the original-intent approach to constitutional interpretation, could the Framers and the states that ratified the Constitution even have conceived of an invention that could move a person at that speed? In their time, the only way to achieve such a speed was to jump off a cliff.

B.   No, because Congress seeks to interfere in matters clearly within the states' police power.

True or false: Congress seeks to interfere in matters clearly within the states' police power?

Au contraire! Congress seeks to control the spending of money that it has appropriated. The states can do what they want.

Setting speed limits is clearly within states' police power; no one disputes that. Congress is not requiring states to set any particular limits; it merely is saying that if states choose to set what Congress deems to be unreasonably high limits, then Congress chooses not to supply highway funding. States have the power to set their own speed limits; they lack the power to compel Congress to support their decisions.

C.   Yes, because Congress has power to do that from the Necessary-and-Proper Clause.

True or false: Congress has power to do that (make eligibility for federal highway funding conditional) from the Necessary-and-Proper Clause?

False, *false, false, FALSE*!! The Necessary-and-Proper Clause is *never* (and we really mean never) a stand-alone source of congressional power. It really functions as an admonition to construe the first seventeen clauses of art. I, § 8, broadly enough to allow Congress reasonable latitude to legislate within the enumerated domains.

D.   No, because art. I, § 8, contains no authorization for Congress to regulate traffic.

True or false: art. I, § 8, contains no authorization for Congress to regulate traffic?

Well, that's certainly true; there is no such authorization, but is Congress asserting the power to regulate traffic? Has Congress said that no one may drive in excess of fifty miles per hour? Certainly not. Congress has said to the states that it will only expend federal highway dollars in a state if the state speed limit is fifty miles per hour or less. There is an authorization allowing Congress to control the federal purse, and no part of the Constitution compels Congress to make any particular expenditures.

As an alternative, this one is overly specific. It invites you to conclude that there is only one way for Congress to legislate to achieve a particular goal. More broadly, it suggests that the Constitution more generally provides only a single way for the government to approach any problem.

Congress is not regulating traffic on the facts of this question. It has not made driving in excess of 50 mph either a civil or criminal offense and has not required any state or local government to make that speed the legal limit. All it has done is effectively to say to the states, "You are entitled to set state speed limits at any level you want, but if you choose a maximum speed that Congress considers unwise, you cannot expect Congress to contribute to your unwise policy."[26]

THE FOLLOWING FACT PATTERN APPLIES TO QUESTIONS ## 4, 5.

Alarmed by skyrocketing divorce rates, a state enacts a statute requiring persons under the age of twenty-five seeking marriage licenses first to receive at least five hours of counseling from a licensed social worker or psychologist. The state's rationale is to provide young lovers information about the nature of marriage and their rights and obligations so they will better understand what marriage is all about.

---

[26] The federal courts have often said that they do not sit to determine the wisdom of legislation, because that is not the courts' job. It *is* the joint job of the legislative and executive branches. (If that sends a chill down your spine, we empathize.)

Suitor, age 23, has successfully proposed to Suitee, also 23,[27] but has not applied for a license because the counseling requirement offends Suitor.

4. If Suitor brings an action in federal court seeking a declaration that the counseling statute is unconstitutional, should the federal court hear the case?

    A. No, because the case presents no substantial federal question within the meaning of the relevant jurisdiction statute.

True or false: the case presents no substantial federal question within the meaning of the relevant jurisdiction statute?

Marriage is one of the few fundamental rights that substantive due process protects. Whether it is constitutionally permissible for a state to burden exercise of the right to marry in this way is certainly a substantial federal question within the meaning of 28 U.S.C. § 1331—even after *Grable* and *Gunn v. Minton*.[28] Note that

---

[27] What happens if only one of the lovebirds is under 25? That might be an interesting interpretive question, but it is not the case with which you are dealing, so you need not consider it. (Besides, there is an easy interpretive answer. The statute does not say that both members of a couple must receive counseling. (Nor does it say that anyone over 25 who wants to marry someone under 25 *must be in need* of some serious counseling, but we digress.))

[28] Please note that we mention the case names only because they *may* ring a bell. If they did not, don't worry about it. You do not need to know case names or otherwise cite cases on the MBE (and, as far as we know, anywhere on any state's bar examination).

In fact, we urge you not to do so in writing essay answers even if you think you can. If you want to refer to a case, do it by a bit of its fact pattern rather than by its name. So you could refer to *Mottley*, for example, as the railroad-passes case. We make this suggestion because over the course of your three or four years, you have read hundreds of cases, and many of them have similar names. For example, in Civil Procedure, you probably read *Grable & Sons Metal Products, Inc. v. Darue Engineering & Mfg. Co.* If you did, you probably remember it as *Grable v. Darue*. You may also have read *Gray v. American Radiator & Std. Sanitary Corp.* If you did, you probably remember it as *Gray v. American Radiator*. Now, those cases have nothing to do with each other; one concerns personal jurisdiction and the other subject-matter jurisdiction. But they both have the same first syllable. In the heat of the moment, you may be thinking of the right case on its facts and legal significance but inadvertently put the name of the other case. If your brain is thinking about the facts and law of *Grable*, but you hurriedly write down *Gray*, we're sorry to tell you that to the grader you will look like an idiot, because the grader does not know you were

this does not mean that a substantive-due-process challenge will necessarily succeed; it may not. But the question does not ask whether Suitor can prevail; it asks only whether the federal court should hear the case, so this cannot be a candidate answer.

B.   Yes, because the right to marry is fundamental.

True or false: the right to marry is fundamental?

It is indeed, but stop and consider the inference that this alternative invites: that the state cannot regulate marriage at all. That is a considerable and unjustified leap. That the right is fundamental clearly does not mean that a state can have no requirements for obtaining a marriage license, such as blood tests, age limitations, and the like. Note that if you were simply scanning the alternatives for a true statement, you might unthinkingly select this one simply because the statement of law is true. Our method is designed in part to discourage you from making such knee-jerk responses. The statement of law *is* true, but that does not dispense with the justiciability requirements for being able to bring a case in a federal court. This is not a candidate answer.

C.   No, because the case presents a non-justiciable political question.

True or false: the case presents a non-justiciable political question?

There is no political question at all here. Marriage rules fall clearly within the domain of state power. There is no textual commitment of such issues to any branch of the federal government, and the state's standard is clear and easily susceptible of judicial interpretation and application. This is not a candidate answer.

---

actually thinking of the correct case. So don't cite cases. Refer to them if you think it is helpful, but do it in an unmistakable way.

D.   No, because the case is not ripe for judicial determination.

True or false: the case is not ripe for judicial determination?

As Hamlet said, "[A]y, there's the rub."[29] Suitor should have proposed and then applied for a marriage license. If the state denied the license, then there would be a ripe controversy, but on the facts as given, the question is purely abstract. This is a candidate answer.

5.   If the federal court, rightly or wrongly in your view, does hear the case, who has the burden of proof?

A.   Suitor, because Suitor is challenging the validity of the state statute, and plaintiffs have the burden of proof in civil cases by a preponderance of the evidence.

True or false: Suitor is challenging the validity of the state statute, and plaintiffs have the burden of proof in civil cases by a preponderance of the evidence?

This is another compound statement, so let's take it apart. The first clause is obviously true, but what about the second clause? Gee, it sounds so familiar—and so it should. But take a closer look: the second clause states an absolute rule. Now ask yourself whether plaintiffs *always* have the burden of proof in civil cases by a preponderance.

This statement is generally true, but not always—and not in this case. This alternative fails to consider a considerable exception to the general plaintiff's-burden rule. If the alternative said, "plaintiffs *always* have the burden of proof in civil cases. . .," you might be more likely to reject it, because then the statement's absoluteness is clearer. Even without that word, however, the alternative still states the proposition absolutely because as worded, it admits of no exceptions.

---

[29]   William Shakespeare, *Hamlet*, act. III, sc. 1.

Marriage is a fundamental right, and cases involving the right to marry come under the strict-scrutiny standard. It is the state's burden to demonstrate both a compelling state interest *and* a narrowly tailored regulation to further the compelling interest in a way that is not unduly restrictive. Note that this does not mean Suitor will prevail on the merits, but defending the statute is the state's hill to climb. This is not a candidate answer.

B. On the state, because the state seeks to pursue an important government interest and must therefore show that the statute is substantially related to achieving the state's goal.

True or false: the state seeks to pursue an important government interest and must therefore show that the statute is substantially related to achieving the state's goal?

Instead of wrestling with whether there is an important state interest (and one might concede that facilitating stable marriages is an important state interest), let's look first at what the state is trying to regulate: marriage. Where does marriage stand in the constitutional hierarchy? Most recently, we know from *Obergefell v. Hodges*, the same-sex marriage case in 2015, that marriage is a fundamental right, the Supreme Court having ruled on the bases of the Due Process and the Equal Protection Clauses. What sort of review do fundamental rights get in constitutional challenges? Right: strict scrutiny. Does this alternative correctly state the test of strict scrutiny?

This is not a candidate answer. It is correct that the burden is on the state here, but the alternative then states the test of intermediate, not strict, scrutiny, so that part of the alternative is not true. Under the weaker burden, the state's chances of prevailing grow.

C. On Suitor, because the combination of the Tenth
    Amendment and the absence of any federal constitutional
    authorization with respect to marriages in the
    Constitution means states have plenary power to regulate
    the conditions for marriages as long as they to not rest
    any condition on membership in a suspect class.

True or false: States have plenary power to regulate marriage
as long as they do not discriminate against a suspect class?

What suspect classes has the Supreme Court recognized? There
are only four: race, religion, national origin, and alienage. Sex and
sexual orientation have not made the list. Does that mean that all
bets are off? Certainly not. This alternative invites sloppy thinking.
There is no suspect class here. Then the question is whether strict-
scrutiny review applies only to suspect classes?

State power with respect to marriage is not plenary; if it were,
same-sex marriage would probably still be unlawful in substantial
parts of the country. Certainly, defining marriage regulations in
terms of a suspect class would almost certainly doom a state
statute, but substantive-due-process rights are more encompassing
than the law of suspect classes. States can, for example, regulate
the ages at which minors can marry, but they cannot regulate the
ages at which adults can marry, nor, for example, can they regulate
the permissible age gap between adults who wish to marry. You may
have heard the expression "May-December marriage" applied to a
couple where one person is much older than the other. Well, as long
as both are adults, the calendar is none of the state's business. This
is not a candidate answer.

D. On the state, because the Due Process and Equal
    Protection Clauses of the Fourteenth Amendment protect
    the right to marry, and the state cannot burden that right
    unless in service of a compelling state interest and in a
    manner that the state tailors narrowly to have the

minimum impact on that right that is consistent with the state's objective.

True or false: (1) the Due Process and Equal Protection Clauses of the Fourteenth Amendment protect the right to marry? Well, that may not have been so clear before *Obergefell*, but it certainly is clear now.

True or false: (2) the state cannot burden that right unless in service of a compelling state interest and in a manner that the state tailors narrowly to have the minimum impact on that right that is consistent with the state's objective. What standard does this part of the alternative state?

This is the best available answer. It places the burden where it belongs and states the burden correctly. Now, it may be that the statute will survive strict scrutiny; it's hard to tell whether a court would find the state's objective sufficiently compelling and the means sufficiently narrowly tailored. (We are skeptical.) But the question does not ask you to make either of those evaluations, and it is important not to let your view of the merits intrude on your answer to the call of the question. Be careful not to factor into your thinking the answer to an unasked question.

* * *

6. A state statute bans sale of contraceptive devices or medications to minors. Distributor sold a contraceptive to X one week before X's 18th birthday. The state charges Distributor, a national retailer of drugs and contraceptive devices, with violation of the statute. Who is likely to prevail?

   A. Distributor, because the statute interferes with a fundamental right.

True or false: the statute interferes with a fundamental right? In studying fundamental rights in your Con Law class, do you recall anything about a fundamental right for minors to purchase contraceptives? If you do, we need to talk. There is a limited number of fundamental rights, but that one is not among them.[30]

This is not a candidate answer. The alternative may call to mind *Griswold v. Connecticut* (1965), but the fundamental right there was marital privacy, not any idea that the Constitution encompasses some sort of right with respect to contraceptives. The Court has never recognized a fundamental right to contraceptives or any other medical devices or drugs.

B.   The state, because Distributor lacks standing to defend the rights of others.

True or false: distributor lacks standing to defend the rights of others?

This alternative is incorrect, though perhaps tempting. As a *general* matter, litigants cannot assert the rights of others. However, in 1976, the Court allowed a beer vendor to challenge a statute on the ground that it violated the equal-protection rights of males under 21. The Court noted that the rule against *jus tertii* (asserting the rights of others) is not a constitutional limitation on the courts' power but rather a self-imposed limitation of lesser stature. The Court found that the statute created injury-in-fact for the vendor by restricting the available market, and allowed the case to go forward. This is not a candidate answer.

C.   Distributor, because the statute denies Distributor a privilege or immunity of citizens of the United States within the meaning of the Fourteenth Amendment.

True or false: the statute denies Distributor a privilege or immunity of citizens of the United States within the meaning of the Fourteenth Amendment?

---

[30]   Never mind whether you think the state's policy is good or bad; certainly one could argue that it is very short-sighted, but the question does not ask you to make that evaluation, and no court should make that evaluation either.

What are the privileges and immunities of federal citizenship? They are far more limited than one might think.

This is not a candidate answer. (In fact, that clause of the Fourteenth Amendment will virtually never be the correct answer to an MBE question.) The Court has held privileges and immunities of "citizens of the United States," encompasses only rights of *federal* citizenship, such as voting in federal elections, petitioning Congress, and interstate travel. It does not even generally protect federal constitutional rights with which the states may not interfere (such as First-Amendment rights); if it did, all of the Court's jurisprudence about the Fourteenth Amendment's Due-Process Clause *incorporating* most of the Bill of Rights would be unnecessary.

> D. The state, because minors' rights do not get the same level of protection against rational state actions that adults' rights get.

True or false: minors' rights do not get the same level of protection against rational state actions that adults' rights get?

This is a correct statement, provided that a court can find that there is a rational basis for the state statute. Recall that that is not hard to do. The burden rests on the challenger to show that there is no rational basis, and the Court has been quite accepting of bases with, shall we say, thin connections to rationality. This statute may exist as the state's attempt to deter recreational sex between minors by making it more difficult to engage in sex without increased risk of conception. There may be lots of rational arguments against that idea as well, but rational-basis review does not require the state's basis to be the *only* rational way—or even the most rational way (a judgment the courts are not entitled to make)—to resolve the perceived difficulty. This is the best available answer.

7.   Citizen, unhappy about a recent city council decision, stood in front of city hall and gave a speech belittling each member of the council. The speech included the following statement: "If there is a god, the city council members will burn in hell forever." An 1898 state criminal statute prohibited "the public utterance of any blasphemy or sacrilege." A police officer arrested Citizen, and the district attorney decided to prosecute, only the third such prosecution in the statute's history. Which of the following arguments would be the least helpful for the defense.

A.   Applying the statute to the Citizen infringes Citizen's freedom of speech in violation of the Fourteenth Amendment.

True or false: applying the statute to the Citizen infringes Citizen's freedom of speech in violation of the Fourteenth Amendment?

This is a plausible argument that invites you to make a knee-jerk mistake. Your first reaction may be that the statutory infirmity falls under the First Amendment, not the Fourteenth. But recall that the First Amendment's protections apply to the states only *through* the Fourteenth Amendment's Due Process Clause. Chief Justice Marshall ruled in 1833 that the Bill of Rights does not apply directly to the states, and the Court has never overruled that decision. Instead, the Court has applied Bill-of-Rights protections to the states through the Fourteenth Amendment, which did not exist when Marshall made his ruling.

As for the statute itself, it clearly addresses itself to the content and viewpoint of speech. Such statutes get strict-scrutiny review, and the state can point to no compelling state interest. One state interest might be favoring of religion over non-religion, but that is unconstitutional. A second state interest might be preventing violence in reaction to a person's statements (the heckler's veto), but punishing the speech clearly is not a narrowly tailored method of pursuing the state's goal of community peace.

At this point, it is important to remember the call of the question. Your job is to identify the *least helpful* argument for Citizen. The freedom-of-speech argument is more than plausible; it is likely to prevail. Therefore this cannot be a candidate answer.

    B.   The statute violates the Fourteenth Amendment because it is an implicit establishment of religion.

True or false: the statute violates the Fourteenth Amendment because it is an implicit establishment of religion?

This is a weaker argument than the preceding alternative, and it is less likely to prevail. The statute addresses the content of speech specifically. Concluding that it is an implicit establishment requires consideration of the legislature's unspoken motive in enacting it. That is a much harder row to hoe; courts are reluctant to consider legislative motives (as distinguished from intent[31]). Nonetheless it is plausible; an attorney could argue the point without embarrassment. This is not a candidate answer.

    C.   Applying the statute to Citizen denies the citizen equal protection of the law.

True or false: applying the statute to Citizen denies the citizen equal protection of the law?

Are there any facts in the record to suggest that the statute does not apply equally to all? This is a candidate answer because there are none. (Remember, we're looking for the *least* helpful argument.) Citizen may be relying on some concept of selective prosecution, but nothing requires the state to prosecute every violation of a statute. Unless Citizen can show a pattern of invidious

---

[31] If you are not clear on the difference between motive and intent, it is this: intent concerns *what* the legislature wanted to accomplish, while motive concerns *why* the legislature wanted to accomplish it.

discrimination in the state's selection of people to prosecute under the statute, a selective-prosecution challenge is dead in the water. Citizen's case is only the third to proceed under the statute, far too small a sample on which to erect an argument of selective prosecution.

D.   The statute violates the Fourteenth Amendment's Due Process Clause because the statute is vague.

True or false: the statute violates the Fourteenth Amendment's Due Process Clause because the statute is vague?

This is not a candidate answer. What is "blasphemy"? What is "sacrilege"? There are many religions in the world, and more than one of those holds that its view is the *only* correct view.[32] Does that mean that its practitioners blaspheme if they espouse that religions other than their own are false?

Vagueness is also a strong argument, whether or not it would prevail on the merits. The statute does not define "blasphemy" or "sacrilege." Some religions affirm the existence of hell and the consignment of souls to it. Was Citizen's statement blasphemy, sacrilege, or preaching?

8.   If Congress thinks that having nationally uniform standards for divorce is essential to prevent unhappily married persons from shopping among the states for "divorce mills"—states with minimal residence requirements and many grounds for divorce—could Congress enact such a statute and have it survive constitutional challenge?

---

[32]   That idea is what makes "conversion" from one religion to another possible. There would be no need for conversion if people could accept the idea that there are many possible views of the nature of a deity. It apparently does not occur to people that if there is a deity and the deity is omnipotent and omniscient, then by definition the deity may choose to present differently to different people—for example, as Allah to followers of Islam, as the Trinity to followers of Christianity, or as Jehovah to followers of Judaism.

A. No, because matters associated with family law—eligibility for marriage, fees, waiting periods, medical tests, and divorce—are within the exclusive province of the states unless the states act inconsistently with the Constitution.

True or false: matters associated with family law—eligibility for marriage, fees, waiting periods, medical tests, and divorce—are within the exclusive province of the states unless the states act inconsistently with the Constitution?

What part of art. I, § 8, gives Congress any power to legislate about either marriage or divorce?

This is a candidate answer. Nothing in the Constitution even suggests that Congress can act in the area of family law. You may recall that the federal courts will decline to exercise diversity jurisdiction over cases involving domestic relations. With the exception of constitutional amendments that may bear on states' exercise of their exclusive power, the Constitution and the federal government are strictly hands-off in this area.

B. Yes, under the Commerce Clause.

True or false: Congress can regulate divorce pursuant to the Commerce Clause?

This is not a candidate answer. The Commerce Clause is broad, but not broad enough to include activity that is clearly not commercial in nature.[33] Divorce, though often attended by great battles over the distribution of assets, is nonetheless not commerce.

C. Yes, under the Police Power.

True or false: Congress can legislate under the Police Power?

---

[33] Cynics, hush up.

What part of art. I, § 8, gives Congress any police power? There is no explicit federal police power. "Police power" is a fuzzy term that the Court has used to characterize a state's entitlement to legislate with respect to the health and safety of its inhabitants. Some of those regulations may have incidental impacts on interstate commerce, but that is permissible. Courts weigh the benefits of state regulations against the burden they impose on interstate commerce. (This is hardly a clear standard, but that is nothing unusual in the law.)

This alternative refers to law that simply does not exist. The police power that the Court has recognized is a creature of state governments.

> D.　No, because Congress cannot pass any legislation not explicitly authorized by U.S. CONST. art. I, § 8, or by a constitutional amendment.

True or false: Congress cannot pass any legislation not explicitly authorized by U.S. CONST. art. I, § 8, or by a constitutional amendment?

You must be careful with this one. What is the key word in this alternative? Why is "explicitly" there?

This statement may be tempting at first glance; that's why you need to go beyond the first glance and your gut reaction. If this alternative were true, there would be nothing for the Necessary-and-Proper Clause, art. I, § 8, cl. 18, to do. That Clause is really a declaration that Congress *can* legislate in areas *not* explicitly mentioned in the first seventeen clauses. It is a rule of constitutional construction as much as a grant of power. Once again, we have an alternative that makes an absolute statement; you should always be suspicious of those, and you can test your suspicion by hypothesizing a situation that does not fit within the absolute statement.[34]

9.   State A's tax law imposed a 20% excise tax on liquor sales but exempted alcoholic beverages produced in State A. Producers from outside State A properly commenced a proceeding in the state's courts, seeking a declaration that the tax was unconstitutional because the exemption for beverages produced in State A violated the Commerce Clause. State courts, from the trial court through the state's supreme court rejected the producers' challenge on the ground that the exemption was rationally related to State A's desire to encourage and support local industry. The United States Supreme Court granted review. How should the Court rule?

A.   The tax is invalid because it violates the Commerce Clause by creating a competitive advantage for State-A beverage producers.

True or false: the tax violates the Commerce Clause by creating a competitive advantage for State-A beverage producers?

This is a candidate answer. The statute discriminates against alcoholic beverages produced out-of-state. The state's desire to support local industry, standing alone, is not objectionable, but it cannot do so by constitutionally impermissible means, such as discriminating against interstate commerce.

B.   The tax is valid because supporting local industry is a permissible state goal.

True or false: the tax is valid because supporting local industry is a permissible state goal?

---

[34] The alternative is false for a second reason as well. Although most delegations of congressional legislative power are in art. I, § 8, and various constitutional amendments, art. IV also confers some legislative jurisdiction. *See* U.S. Const. art. IV, § 1 and § 3 cl. 2.

This is not a candidate answer. To say that the goal is permissible is not to say that any and all means of pursuing the goal are necessarily permissible. Ends do not justify means, so pursuing the goal by unconstitutional methods is illegitimate.

C.   The tax is invalid because it denies equal protection of the laws.

True or false: the tax denies equal protection of the laws?

This is a possible argument and not a bad one, but it is more difficult to make than the Commerce-Clause argument. It is not as good an argument because the plaintiffs will have the burden of proof. There is no suspect or quasi-suspect class here, so the court will apply rational-basis analysis. Thus, the plaintiffs will have to show that there is no rational basis, and they will have to argue that the tax serves no permissible state purpose. They might prevail, but the case for discrimination against interstate commerce is much easier to make. Therefore this is not a candidate answer.

D.   The tax is valid because government subsidies are permissible, and the tax is a *de facto* subsidy to State-A beverage producers.

True or false: government subsidies are permissible?

It certainly is true that government subsidies are permissible, but with a strong *proviso*. Subsidies are permissible *only* if they do not violate some provision of the Constitution. Taxing only non-State-A-beverage sales puts their producers at a competitive disadvantage *vis-à-vis* State-A beverage producers and thus violates the Commerce Clause. The Commerce Clause does allow state laws to have incidental effects on commerce, but this tax is direct and by no means incidental.

Contracts

1. Owner posted a notice on a community bulletin board outside the local hardware store stating, "Paint my house white by the end of August. Will pay $5,000 plus expenses. Call 321-1234."

    Painter saw the notice, searched on-line for the phone number, and found Owner's name and address. Painter drove past the house and estimated how much paint it needed. Painter then bought the necessary paint and supplies.

    The next morning, Painter drove to Owner's house and set up his work materials. Owner ran out of the house, telling Painter to stop. Unbeknownst to Painter, Second Painter had called Owner the prior evening, and the two had agreed that Second Painter would paint the house the following week. Who has a contract to paint Owner's house?

    A. Painter, because Owner's notice was an offer of a unilateral contract, and Painter accepted by partial performance when he purchased the paint and showed up at the house.

    True or false: Owner's notice was an offer of a unilateral contract, and Painter accepted by partial performance when he purchased the paint and showed up at the house?

    Remember that the first step with any compound conjunctive statement is to break it apart. True or false: Owner offered a unilateral contract?

    A unilateral contract offer must specifically call for acceptance by performance, not promise. Owner clearly wants the house painted. But the offer specifies a would-be painter's next step: "Call 321-1234." Owner was offering a bilateral contract, since one of the terms of the offer required the offeree to do something other than perform. So that part of the alternative's statement is not true, meaning that this alternative cannot be correct.

We could stop there, but let's not. Remember that what we are working on together is the technique of arriving at an answer, not simply whether a particular answer is right or wrong. If it is wrong, what makes it wrong?

True or false: Painter partially performed by purchasing paint and going to Owner's house?

This is an answer that your gut may jump at, but it is incorrect. Under the modern rule, partial performance accepts an offer of a unilateral contract, *but* mere preparation, such as purchasing supplies or setting up to paint is *not* partial performance. There must be at least some of Painter's paint *on* the house, not merely *at* the house. Painter had not begun painting, so there was no partial performance when Owner withdrew the offer by telling Painter to stop.

At this point you may be wondering why you should bother with this part of the analysis. There really are two reasons. First, this is review, so analyzing the second part of the alternative reviews another principle of contract law. Second, what if your analysis of the first part of a compound conjunctive alternative is incorrect? That kind of alternative must be entirely correct to be right answer.[35] Analyzing both parts of the statement gives you a fallback in case you are incorrect about one part.   ·

   B.   Second Painter, because Second Painter and Owner
        agreed to a bilateral contract.

---

[35] Note that, as we mentioned, this sort of approach does not necessarily apply to best/worst/least/most kinds of questions. There you may have more than one alternative that, standing alone, is correct, but it may not as good an answer to the question as some other alternative.

This is clearly correct; the question tells you that in so many words. Bilateral contracts require no performance (or even preparation) to make the contact binding.

C.   Painter, because he began performance before Owner's statement of revocation.

Is that alternative true or false?

In the case of unilateral offers, the modern rule is that partial performance is a valid acceptance, *but* mere preparation, such as purchasing supplies or setting up to paint is *not* partial performance. There must be at least some of Painter's paint *on* the house, not merely *at* the house. Painter had not begun painting, so even if one thinks Owner offered a unilateral contract, there was no partial performance when Owner withdrew the offer by telling Painter to stop.

D.   Second Painter, because Painter had not commenced performance.

True or false: Second Painter has a contract because Painter had not commenced performance?

It is true that Second Painter has a contract. It is also true that Painter had not commenced performance. So why isn't this an acceptable answer? That troublesome word "because" is the problem here. Second Painter has a contact because Second Painter and Owner formed a bilateral contract by an exchange of promises. Second Painter does not have a contract *because* Painter had not commenced performance.

Consider it this way. If Owner's offer was for a unilateral contract, and if Owner and Second Painter never had spoken on the telephone, would Owner telling Painter to stop and go home create a contract between Owner and Second Painter? Of course not.

2. Landowner telephoned Fencer on February 1, 2019, and asked Fencer to fence and cross-fence 1,000 acres into 10-acre fields by May 1, 2019, for $500 per acre, including materials. Landowner told Fencer not to use barbed wire. Fencer accepted, and they hung up. On April 14, 2019, Fencer filed for bankruptcy. By April 20, 2019, Fencer had completed 500 acres. Landowner learned of the bankruptcy filing on April 21 and told Fencer he was fired. Landowner then hired someone else to complete the fencing.

    What is a justifiable ground for Landowner's terminating Fencer?

    A.   Fencer had only completed 50% of the job by April 20.

    True or false: Fencer had only completed 50% of the job by April 20?

    That is obviously true, but that does not mean that, having found a true statement, you should leap at this alternative. What did the contract require of Fencer? Fencer had to complete the job by May 1. On April 21, when Landowner purported to terminate the contract, was Fencer in breach?

    A is not a candidate answer, because Fencer was not in breach. Neither party to a contract can repudiate it unless the other contracting party is in breach. If the law were otherwise, every contract would be the equivalent of the illusory contract that you heard about: "I will if I want to." The whole point of contracts being binding before performance (or, in the case of unilateral contracts, before complete performance) is to prevent that uncertainty in business dealings.

    B.   Fencer had filed for bankruptcy on April 14.

    True or false: Landowner was justified in terminating Fencer because Fender had filed for bankruptcy on April 14?

Terminating a contract early requires an existing breach of a material term of the contract. Is filing for bankruptcy a material breach of the contract between Landowner and Fencer? How could it be unless the contract explicitly made not filing for bankruptcy a material term? Fencer's seeking bankruptcy protection is not a breach of the contract, and Fencer may be able to complete the fencing in the required time. Landowner may have anticipated that Fencer would not be able to meet the May 1 date, but that does not make Fencer in breach.[36] B is not a candidate answer.

C.   If Fencer had used barbed wire.

True or false: Landowner was justified in terminating the contract with Fencer because Fencer used barbed wire when the contract specified that Fencer use no barbed wire?

C is a candidate answer. If Fencer had used barbed wire, that was a breach of a material term of the contract: installing the one type of wire that the contract specifically prohibited. That would justify Landowner terminating the contract.

D.   The contract was not in writing.

True or false: Landowner was justified in terminating the contract because it was not in writing?

Note the implication of this alternative: that *all* contracts need to be in writing. This is another absolute statement, and like most absolute statements about the law, it is not true. The statement does not contain "absolute," but neither does it recognize the possibility of exceptions—in this situation rather broad exceptions— to the rule that it states.

---

[36] An important lesson: (filing for bankruptcy protection) ≠ death. Filing does not render the filer non-functional.

Focus on what types of contracts need to be in writing. For example, the UCC requires written agreements for sales of goods. Installing fences is not a sale of goods.

The Statute of Frauds requires written agreements if it is not possible to perform the contract within one year. Here it was not only possible to perform within a year; the contract's terms demanded performance in less than a year.

The law of property requires written agreements for sales of land. There is no transfer of real property here.

D is not a candidate answer.

3.   Plaintiff lived across the street from an auto body shop. One evening, Plaintiff saw several people trying to break into the shop's office. Plaintiff called 911 and then went out and yelled at the intruders. They fled, but police later apprehended them. The next day, the owner of the shop stopped by to thank Plaintiff and told Plaintiff that the shop would detail Plaintiff's car once a year for as long as Plaintiff owned it.

The shop detailed Plaintiff's car for two years, but in the third year the shop owner told Plaintiff that he would have to pay for the detailing. If Plaintiff sues to enforce the owner's promise, who will prevail?

A.   Plaintiff, because the shop had already commenced performance of the promise in the two previous years.

True or false: the shop had already commenced performance of the promise in the two previous years?

Well, certainly it is true, but that is not the real issue. The questions are (1) whether the promise was enforceable when made and, (2) if not, whether commencing performance made the promise enforceable. Commencing performance sometimes creates a contract—a unilateral contract. Is there a unilateral contract here?

Contracts require offer and acceptance. What is the offer here? If you are thinking that the owner's promise was an offer of a unilateral contract, then what is the acceptance?

This is not a candidate answer. A promise, standing alone, does not form a contract. It doesn't form a contract even if the promisee says, "Thank you." There must be consideration on both sides. Owner made the promise based on what Plaintiff had already done; that is *past* consideration, and the law of contracts does not recognize past consideration as a basis for a contract. Owner's promise was gratuitous and so not enforceable. Owner's having honored the gratuitous promise twice did not create the consideration missing from Plaintiff's side and so did not change the gratuitous nature of the promise.

B.   Owner, because Plaintiff's actions on the night of the attempted break-in were not pursuant to any implied contract between the parties and were merely gratuitous. When Plaintiff acted, there was no consideration for Plaintiff's actions and so no contract arose.

True or false: When Plaintiff acted, there was no consideration for Plaintiff's actions and so no contract arose?

This is a candidate answer. Plaintiff is a wonderful person. All hail Plaintiff. But Plaintiff's actions were entirely gratuitous; they could not unilaterally create any obligation on Owner's part. Owner's promise, coming after Plaintiff's actions, is a promise based on past consideration. That may make Owner also a wonderful person, but past consideration does not form a contract.

C.   Plaintiff, because Plaintiff had had no duty to intervene, and Plaintiff's decision to do so constituted consideration.

True or false: because Plaintiff had had no duty to intervene . . . Plaintiff's decision to do so constituted consideration?

Yep, it's another one of those compound alternatives, so here we go. True or false: Plaintiff had had no duty to intervene? As a general matter, there is no legal obligation to be a laudable person.[37] That part of the alternative is correct.

True or false: Plaintiff's decision to intervene constituted consideration?

Time to hit the "Pause" button. Consideration for what? Owner had made no offer when Plaintiff acted. Plaintiff had not made an offer either. Why is consideration even relevant? Now, had Plaintiff and Owner agreed beforehand that *if* Plaintiff took action to protect the shop, *then* Owner would detail Plaintiff's car annually at no charge for as long as Plaintiff owned it, Plaintiff's *subsequent* intervention would have constituted acceptance of Owner's offer of a unilateral contract. Here the intervention preceded the promise, and that sequence produces no contract.

Think of the implications were the rule otherwise. In the absence of any offer, a single person could create a contract with another simply by doing something to benefit the other. The good Samaritan deserves respect, and the Samaritan's voluntary actions may create a moral obligation, but they do not create a legal obligation.

D.   Owner, because there was no written agreement between Plaintiff and Owner.

True or false: there was no written agreement between Plaintiff and Owner?

There certainly wasn't. There was no contract at all between Plaintiff and Owner. If there had been an offer and acceptance, with consideration on both sides, then the resultant contract would have

---

[37] Yes, yes; if someone does something unjustifiable that places someone else in jeopardy, a duty to intervene to prevent the harm arises. Good for you for remembering! But that is not part of this question.

had to be in writing because Owner could not perform it within a year.

However, this is not a candidate answer. The problem in this question is that there was no agreement between the parties when Plaintiff acted, and Plaintiff's actions were not in response to any offer by Owner. They were gratuitous. In turn, Owner's promise to Plaintiff after the dust had settled was also gratuitous, since a contract cannot form based on past consideration.

4.   Hardware-store Owner contracted with Genco for Genco to provide four Model X generators per month at a price of $3,000 per generator. For six months, Genco delivered the generators, and Owner paid $12,000 each month. Then the local power utility announced that it would shut down power from time to time to lessen the danger during the fire season. Owner e-mailed Genco saying that it was an emergency and that Genco should deliver as many generators as it could for the remainder of the fire season. Genco emailed back that it could deliver more but that they might cost more than $3,000 per machine. Genco delivered five additional generators the following month and charged $4,000 each for them. Owner wanted them, so Owner paid the total to Genco. If Owner now sues to recoup $5,000, who is likely to prevail?

   A.   Owner, because there was already a contract pricing generators at $3,000 each.

True or false: Owner will prevail because there was a pre-existing contract pricing generators at $3,000 each?

Yes, there was already a contract pricing generators at $3,000 each, but it specified four generators per month at that price. It was not a contract to sell as many generators per month as Owner might request. That contract has not gone away. The parties modified that contract in writing (because it is a contract for the sale of goods) with their exchange of emails for a supply of additional generators. They did not agree on a price, but UCC § 2-305 covers that, directing that the court set a "reasonable price." It may be that $4,000 is not a reasonable price, but that does not mean that, given the changed circumstances, that $3,000 is or that, even if it is, it is the *maximum* reasonable price. Reasonability does not have fixed, easily discernible boundaries (which is why it drove us all nuts in Torts). Owner may prevail totally or partially, but Owner certainly will not prevail *because of* the $3,000 per generator price for the first four generators. This is not a candidate answer.

> B.   Genco, because Owner said it was an emergency, so Genco was free to raise the price.

True or false: Owner said it was an emergency, so Genco was free to raise the price?

Break it down. True or false: Owner said it was an emergency? Certainly.

True or false: Genco was free to raise the price?

This is not a candidate answer either because it is overbroad. It is another absolute statement, suggesting that pricing for the additional units was unilaterally within Genco's control. Would you enter into such a contract? Price is a material term in any contract. What happens if the contract does not contain any price?

The emails recognized there was an emergency; that's what generated (so to speak) Owner's need for more units. But UCC § 2-305 limits the seller to a reasonable price for the additional goods. This alternative improperly suggests that there were no limits on seller's discretion in charging more.

> C.   Owner, because there was no written instrument altering the terms of the original contract.

True or false: Owner prevails because there was no written instrument altering the terms of the original contract?

For grammarians, at least, the "because" statement is true; there was no *single* written instrument altering the terms of the original contract. The implication, of course, is that modifications (and perhaps all written contracts?) must be in a single instrument. Is that true?

This is not a candidate answer, because email (or snail mail) exchanges can be effective to form or modify a written contract. A valid written contract need not appear in a single document.[38] An offer may arrive by mail, and the offeree may accept by return mail.[39] That being the case, the parties can modify an existing written contract by a later written exchange.

D.   Genco, because the exchange of emails was a valid modification of the original contract, provided that $4,000 was a reasonable price for the additional generators.

True or false: the exchange of emails was a valid modification of the original contract, provided that $4,000 was a reasonable price for the additional generators?

This is a correct statement of the law. Note that this alternative does not ask you to determine whether $4,000 was a reasonable price in the circumstances, and you have no basis on which to do so. Avoid taking on decision burdens that the question does not force on you.

---

[38] We hasten to add that both lawyers' and clients' lives are much easier if there *is* a single document containing the entire agreement. As a matter of practice, that is more desirable.

[39] That's where one has to consider whether a state follows the dispatch or receipt rule.

Property

1.   A and B purchased an apartment together as joint tenants with right of survivorship. They recorded the properly executed deed promptly. Several months later, A executed a deed for the apartment to C, forging B's name. C promptly recorded the deed. To whom does the apartment now belong?[40]

A.   A and B as joint tenants with right of survivorship.

True or false: It still belongs to A and B as joint tenants with right of survivorship?

This alternative really says that no joint tenant acting unilaterally can affect title to property that is held in joint tenancy. At common law, that was true. Traditionally, a forged instrument was null. However, the modern rule recognizes "partial validity," where one party can convey the party's own interest. In this case, A could convey A's interest to C but could not convey B's interest. That means that A and B are no longer joint tenants. More than that, the conveyance destroys the joint tenancy, because joint tenancies must arise from a single transaction; the tenants cannot acquire their titles sequentially. This is not a candidate answer.

B.   C and B as joint tenants with right of survivorship.

True or false: It belongs to C and B as joint tenants with right of survivorship?

This may be an appealing answer because one is apt to think that A has simply substituted C in A's place. Logically, that makes some sense. But, as Justice Holmes warned us long ago, "The life of the law has not been logic: it has been experience." This is not a candidate answer because the partial conveyance severed the joint tenancy and created a tenancy-in-common in its place. Joint

---

[40] Before attempting to answer a question like this, organize in your mind (or on scrap paper) what the elements of the various freehold estates are. This will make your analysis of each alternative sharper (and shorter).

tenancies must arise at the same time from the same instrument; C's and B's tenancies meet neither of these requirements.

C.   C and B as tenants in common.

True or false: The apartment belongs to C and B as tenants in common?

This is a correct answer under the modern rule. A's conveyance of A's interest to C is valid. Obviously, A's fraudulent attempt to convey B's interest is not valid. So B and C now own the property. But how do they hold it? They cannot be joint tenants because their interests did not arise at the same time through a single conveyance. They cannot be tenants by the entirety for two reasons. First, as far as we know, they are not married, and that is a bit of a problem. (Being married is also sometimes a bit of a problem, but we digress.) Even if they got married after A and B divorced or A died, there would still be no tenancy by the entirety because their interests vested at different times through different instruments.

D.   C in fee simple.

This is not a candidate answer under either the modern or the common-law rule. A could not transfer B's interest without B's consent, so A could not convey fee simple. Under the common-law approach, the instrument purporting to transfer title to C would have no effect whatsoever; A and B would remain joint tenants.[41] Under the modern rule, A transferred A's interest in the property, leaving B's interest *almost* untouched. Why "almost"? A's transfer to C ruptured the joint tenancy between A and B, and one of the casualties of that was B's right of survivorship. That has disappeared.

---

[41]   B, at that point, clearly would have developed a strong reason to bring to rapid fruition the survivorship right that B enjoyed.

2. Owner had an apartment building. Tenant signed a two-year lease for an apartment at $750 per month. Tenant promptly paid the rent each month for the entire lease period and for three months after that, at which point Owner had a notice of eviction served on Tenant. What is Tenant's strongest argument to prevent eviction?

   A. Owner did not evict Tenant at the end of the two-year lease term.

   True or false: Owner did not evict Tenant at the end of the two-year lease term? Well, that's kind of a gimme, isn't it? The real issue is whether eviction at the end of a term of years is a now-or-never proposition, because that's what this alternative suggests. What is the likelihood of Tenant prevailing on that argument?

   This is not a candidate answer. Owner's inaction when the lease term ended merely converted the lease from a fixed term to a monthly periodic tenancy; it didn't forever extinguish Owner's right to wrest the property from Tenant's control. A periodic tenancy continues indefinitely, subject to its proper termination by either party.

   B. By allowing Tenant to continue living in the apartment, Owner allowed another yearly lease to form, preventing Owner from terminating it mid-year.

   True or false: by allowing Tenant to continue living in the apartment, Owner allowed another yearly lease to form, preventing Owner from terminating it mid-year?

   This is not a candidate answer. New leases do not form spontaneously. Leases of real property require written agreements. So it is not correct that upon expiration of the two-year lease, another simply leapt into being by virtue of Tenant's continued payments or by Owner's acceptance of those payments. Even leases running year to year convert into monthly periodic tenancies at the end of the lease period. The monthly periodic tenancy is not a lease; it is a form of grace period that the law provides to protect holdover tenants from being evicted overnight.

C.   Tenant had never violated any terms of the original lease, so Owner had no grounds for eviction.

True or false: Tenant had never violated any terms of the original lease, so Owner had no grounds for eviction?

Break it down. True or false: Tenant had never violated any terms of the original lease? Nothing in the facts suggests Tenant had.

True or false: therefore, Owner had no grounds for eviction?

Think about what this alternative really says: as long as Tenant is well-behaved within the meaning of the original lease agreement and continues to tender monthly rent payments, Owner is without power to recover control of the leased property. Really? If that were true, why would anyone need rent control?

This is not a candidate answer. Certainly, if Tenant had never violated any terms of the original lease, Owner could not have sought to evict Tenant during the lease period. But Tenant's good behavior did not operate to amend a material term of the original lease: two years. So on expiration of the two-year period, the law converted the unrenewed two-year tenancy to a periodic month-to-month tenancy. A periodic tenancy is terminable by either party by giving notice of termination, and termination of a periodic tenancy requires no grounds.

D.   Owner had not given Tenant any notice of termination and so could not proceed with eviction when Owner did.

True or false: owner had not given Tenant any notice of termination? One of the most basic rules of answering multiple-choice questions is that if the facts don't say something happened, it didn't happen.

True or false: so Owner could not proceed with eviction when Owner did?

Note the qualification this alternative contains. It does not say Owner cannot evict at all; it merely says that when (and how) Owner attempted eviction, Owner did not then have the right to do that.

This is a correct answer. There is no question that Owner can terminate the tenancy, but that must happen in the proper manner. The law requires notice of termination to precede eviction. The length of the notice may vary from state to state.

3.   Owner has a 100-acre tract of land. Owner conveys 50 acres to Husband and Wife. The deed reads: "To Husband and Wife as tenants by the entirety, and not as joint tenants or tenants in common." Husband and Wife record the deed.

Later, Owner sells the remaining 50 acres to Husband and Friend. That deed reads: "To Husband and Friend as joint tenants and not as tenants in common." Husband and Friend record the deed.

Husband subsequently unilaterally conveys to Relative all Husband's rights, titles, and interests in the two parcels. Then Husband dies. What does Relative own?[42]

A.   An undivided half interest in the second parcel as a tenant-in-common, which has no right of survivorship.

This is a compound alternative, so let's break it up. True or false: tenants in common have no right of survivorship? Well, that's true; that is what distinguishes tenancy in common from joint tenancy.

---

[42] Any time you see multiple transactions like this, do yourself a favor. Make a time-line of the sequence of transactions. We think that is critical to understanding who conveyed what to whom.

Now for the second part. True or false: Relative has an undivided half interest in the second parcel?

There is an unprinted word that nonetheless is part of this alternative: "only." There are two parcels involved here, so you should break down the transaction into its two parts. Was Husband in a position to convey an interest in the second parcel? A joint tenant is entitled to alienate the tenant's interest. Joint tenancy is not an albatross, but the conveyance ruptures the joint tenancy and creates a tenancy in common, which has no right of survivorship.

Now let's turn to the first parcel, the one that Husband and Wife held as tenants by the entirety. Could Husband, acting unilaterally, terminate the entirety and extinguish Wife's right of survivorship? This gets to a critical difference between tenancy by the entirety and joint tenancy.

This is a candidate answer. The right of survivorship attaches to a tenancy by the entirety, and neither spouse can act alone while the marriage lasts to sever the tenancy or defeat the right of survivorship. This distinguishes tenancy by the entirety from joint tenancy. Thus, Husband could not unilaterally convey or otherwise encumber any part of the original 50-acre parcel. Therefore, upon Husband's death, Wife (all right—Widow) owned the 50 acres in fee simple.

The 50-acre second parcel that Husband and Friend held in joint tenancy converted to a tenancy in common for Friend and Relative when Husband conveyed his interest to Relative, with each holding an undivided one-half interest in that parcel as a tenant in common, title in the original parcel remaining with Wife.

B. An undivided one-third interest in the two parcels.

True or false: Relative owns an undivided one-third interest in the two parcels?

This alternative posits that a tenant by the entirety can unilaterally affect the spouses' joint interest in the estate, but that's what differentiates tenancy by the entirety from garden-variety joint tenancy.

This is not a candidate answer. Husband and Wife owned the original parcel as tenants by the entirety. Tenancies by the entirety end by the spouses' joint conveyance, by divorce, or by death of a spouse. There was no joint conveyance here and no divorce. Therefore, the tenancy by the entirety continued until Husband's death, at which time title in the first parcel vested wholly in Wife. Relative takes nothing of the first parcel.

C.   An undivided half interest in the entire 100-acre tract.

True or false: Relative takes an undivided half interest in the entire 100-acre tract?

This is incorrect because Husband and Wife held their parcel as tenants by the entirety with right of survivorship. There are only three ways to end such a tenancy: (1) Husband and Wife agreeing jointly to convey their entire interest to someone else, (2) divorce, in which case the tenancy by the entirety converts into a tenancy in common between Husband and Wife, or (3) death of one of the parties, which vests title in the surviving spouse. Before Husband's death, Relative could acquire an interest in the first parcel only if Husband and Wife acting together deeded an interest to Relative.

D.   An undivided three-quarter interest in the 100-acre tract.

This is incorrect. Relative never acceded to any interest in the original parcel because Husband acted unilaterally. A unilateral act by one spouse has no effect on the tenancy by the entirety (unless the unilateral act is death).

4.   Owner held a 20-acre farm in fee simple, on which he grew and harvested corn. Dude Ranch owned the property abutting the farm on the north. A 300-acre county park was on the farm's

southern border. Dude Ranch had no direct access to the park, so it had to drive its customers and horses to the park.[43]

Twenty-five years ago, Owner built a dirt road running the north/south length of the property to facilitate working the land. Several years later, Dude Ranch began regularly leading horses and riders down the dirt road to get to the park. Whenever Owner was working adjoining fields, Owner would wave to the riders.

Last year, Owner died, leaving his 20-acre farm to Child. Child wanted to subdivide the farm into two-acre housing tracts. When Child saw riders on the dirt road, Child informed them that they were trespassing and could not use the dirt road. Dude Ranch said it had acquired an easement over the dirt road and would continue to use it. Child filed an appropriate action to enjoin Dude Ranch from using the dirt road.

If Child prevails, it will be because Dude Ranch's use of the road was:[44]

A.   Permissive.

True or false: Child may prevail because Dude Ranch's use of the road was permissive?

And here we get to the question of Note 44. What are the possibilities for Dude Ranch's insulation from the injunction that Child seeks? There never was any formal conveyance of an interest by Owner, so what does that leave? The only realistic possibility is that Dude Ranch acquired an easement by prescription. An easement by prescription has four elements: (1) it must be adverse

---

[43] As horse owners, we can tell you that that certainly can be done, but it is a bit of a nuisance each day, for each ride, having to load the horses on a trailer, drive (carefully) to the site of the ride, offload the horses, and then reverse the process at the end of the ride.

[44] If Dude Ranch has an enforceable interest, how did Dude Ranch acquire that interest? What are the elements of the means of acquisition of such an interest? These are questions you should be asking yourself before even looking at the alternatives.

to the use to which the owner of the land puts the easement's portion of the land; (2) it must be open and notorious; (3) it must be continuous, and (4) it must be at least as long as the period required for prescription. Owner always waved to the riders. What does that tell us about these elements? Dude Ranch's use of the dirt road clearly did not satisfy the adversity requirement. The fact that we do not know the required length of the prescriptive period does not matter, since an easement by prescription must satisfy all four elements.

B.   Not continuous.

True or false: Child may prevail because Dude Ranch's use of the road was not continuous?

That depends on what "continuous" means, does it not? It certainly is not that the use must be 24/7. What does it mean? Continuous use means use over a period of time without interference by the owner, either by physically blocking access or by bringing an action against the trespasser to prevent continued access before the trespassory use has ripened into an easement by prescription.

This is not a candidate answer, because nothing in the fact pattern suggests that there was any interruption in Dude Ranch's use of the dirt road, and certainly Owner took no steps to prevent Dude Ranch's access. To the contrary, Owner apparently welcomed Dude Ranch's use.

C.   Not open and notorious.

True or false: Child may prevail because Dude Ranch's use of the road was not open and notorious?

There is a conjunction in this alternative, so be sure to break it down. Was Dude Ranch's use of the road open or was it surreptitious? Given that Owner regularly waived to the riders, that question is pretty much of a no-brainer. What about notorious? If a use is sufficiently regular to impute knowledge of the intrusion to the property owner, then the use is notorious.

Dude Ranch's use of the road probably was notorious. Dude Ranch's use of the road was "regular," so apart from Owner's apparent acceptance of the use, the use was sufficiently routine as to make it fair to consider even an absent owner on constructive notice. So this alternative fails on both grounds.

D.   Not long enough.

True or false: Child may prevail because Dude Ranch did not use the road for a sufficiently long time?

Although this answer is conceivable in the abstract, there is nothing in the facts to support the argument. All we know is that Dude Ranch began using the dirt road "several years" after Owner built it. The typical prescription period is twenty years, although some states have established shorter ones. So whether Child can prevail with this argument depends on an unknown—whether Dude Ranch has used the road for more or less than whatever prescriptive period applies in the state. You were merely guessing if you chose this alternative.

5.   A and B own a parcel of land as joint tenants. B conveys 40% of B's interest to C. Who now owns the property?

A.   A and B own 60% as tenants in common, and A and C own 40% as tenants in common.

Nuts—another compound alternative!

True or false: A and B own 60% as tenants in common?

For this to be true, B's conveyance of a 40% interest to C would have to rupture the joint tenancy for the remaining 60%. Did it? Well, no; the four unities of a joint tenancy[45] for the remaining 60%

---

[45]   (1) The joint tenants must take their share at the same time. (2) The joint tenants must acquire their title from the same instrument. (3) Each joint tenant must

still exist with respect to A and B. One part of this compound alternative is not correct, so the alternative cannot be a candidate answer. But we're doing review here, so let's continue to the second part.

True or false: A and C own 40% as tenants in common?

Without thinking about other possible answers (because you should not be doing that, *see supra* page 12) focus on just this alternative. This part of the alternative is correct. B's conveyance to C ruptures the joint tenancy of A and B with respect to that part of the property, because A and C now have interests, but those interests did not arise at the same time and through the same instrument.

B.   A, B, and C as tenants in common.

True or false: the three parties are tenants in common?

This requires you to know what creates and what terminates a joint tenancy. Joint tenancies come into existence in only one way— through a single instrument vesting undivided title in multiple persons. They end only in one of two ways. Either one (or more or all) of the joint tenants conveys an interest to some new party, or one of the joint tenants dies. A and B still own 60% of the property as joint tenants. B's conveyance to C leaves the joint tenancy untouched (just smaller), and A retains A's interest in the conveyed 40% of the land, though A holds that interest only as a tenant in common with C because joint tenants must take undivided and equal interests in the property by the same instrument at the same time.

C.   A and B own 60% of the property as joint tenants. A and C own 40% of the property as joint tenants.

---

have exactly the same interest as each other tenant. (4) Each joint tenant must have an equal entitlement to the entire property. (This is not true of tenants in common.) Thus, the four unities are time, title, interest, and possession.

True or false: A and B own 60% of the property as joint tenants. A and C own 40% of the property as joint tenants?

This is a compound alternative, so let's consider it piece by piece.

B has done nothing to sever the joint tenancy in 60% of the land. It continues undisturbed.

The second piece, however, is not correct. Joint tenancy comes into existence only by a simultaneous vesting of the joint tenants' undivided title by a single instrument. A's title in the property antedates C's, so joint tenancy with C is not possible.

    D.   A and B own 60% of the property as joint tenants. A and C own 40% of the property as tenants in common.

True or false: A and B own 60% of the property as joint tenants, and A and C own 40% of the property as tenants in common?

Remember: piece by piece. True or false: A and B own 60% of the property as joint tenants?

This is a true statement. B's conveyance of a portion of B's interest in the land is valid, but it does not affect either B's or A's title to the remainder of the land.

True or false: A and C own 40% of the property as tenants in common. This statement is also correct. B can convey a partial or total amount of B's interest to C, but B cannot thus create a joint tenancy because A's and C's titles will have vested at different times by different instruments. B cannot, as it were, substitute C as a joint tenant.

6.   D owns a parcel of land. In January, 2018, D gave E a mortgage on the property to secure a $125,000 loan from E to D. In March, 2018, D gave F a mortgage on the property to secure a $150,000 loan from F to D. In July, 2018, D gave G a mortgage on the property to secure a $100,000 loan from G to D. G

recorded the mortgage. Later that month, E recorded E's mortgage. D never made any payments on any of the mortgages. E, F, and G jointly commenced a foreclosure proceeding and prevailed. At auction, the property sold for $300,000.

The recording statute provides that "any written instrument affecting title to land that is not recorded is void against a subsequent purchaser in good faith for valuable consideration whose conveyance shall be recorded first."

How much can F take from the foreclosure proceeding?

A.   Nothing, because F never recorded D's mortgage.

True or false: F never recorded D's mortgage? That one even Don can answer.

Look at the unspoken premise. *Is* an unrecorded mortgage void?

This alternative is incorrect, but why? How should we think about this problem? The land sale brought $300,000, but the sum of the mortgages is $375,000. The difficulty, obviously, is F's failure to record.

What is the effect of the failure to record? Does it nullify the unrecorded instrument? Under the statute given, it does not. This is why it is critical to read very carefully. The sloppy reader will skim the statute, see and stop at "is not recorded is void," and choose at this alternative. But the statute has no effect on the *validity* of the instrument. It affects only mortgagees' places in line.

G recorded first; that makes G first in line. E, although not recording before G, nonetheless did record. E, therefore, is second in line. F, having never recorded, brings up the rear, but the mortgage is still a valid lien on the land, so F will take whatever is left after G and E have recovered.

B. $75,000.

True or false: F can recover $75,000, though it is only half the amount that F lent D?

Mortgages have priority according to the sequence in which the mortgagees record them. Recorded documents take precedence over unrecorded documents. The dates of the mortgage agreements themselves are irrelevant. (That is why, whenever there is a recordable instrument, the holder should record it promptly.) The sequence of recordation here is G and E (or, if you prefer, G, E, and never.) The question asks how much F can take. Well, we know that G and E take before F. Of the $300,000 proceeds from the foreclosure, G will take $100,000. Next, E will take $150,000. What is left for F? $300,000 – $100,000 – $125,000 = $75,000. This is the correct answer.

C. $150,000.

True or false: F can recover the full amount of F's loan to D?

That is the amount of F's mortgage, of course, but when there are more creditors than assets, what happens? Well, the creditors have to get in line. What determines their places in line? For some transactions, it is the date on which the transactions occurred, a variation of "first come, first served." But the state has altered that rule by statute, under which the relevant factor in establishing priority (place in line) is the date of recordation, not the date on which the debts arose. F, having never recorded, stands last in line. If the land had brought enough to cover all three mortgages, F could have recovered the entire $150,000, but it did not. After G (who recorded first) and E (next) take their shares—for each of them the full amounts of their loans—F finally gets to the front of the line. How much money is still there? Oops.

D. $100,000.

True or false: F can recover $100,000?

Where did this number come from? It isn't the amount of the loan from F to D. (It is the amount of the loan from G to D, but so what?) Because E and G recorded and F did not, under the statute E and G have priority over F. That's all the statute does. Do not misread it to say that it affects the *validity* of an unrecorded instrument; it does not say that. It says only that an unrecorded "instrument affecting title to land that is not recorded is void *against a subsequent purchaser* in good faith for valuable consideration whose conveyance shall be recorded first." [Emphasis added.] What does that language mean? Well for the subsequent good-faith recording purchaser, it is as if the unrecorded instrument is not there at all. But that "voidness" affects only the relationship of the two mortgages to each other.

If F had recorded promptly, F would precede G in line, and G would not be able to "cut the line" to get in front of F. But G recorded, and F did not. For G, the statute says that F isn't in the line in front of G. (And for G, since E recorded later, E isn't in the line in front of G, but E does precede F.) Note that the statute does not cancel the mortgage that F holds. F is still entitled to recover $150,000 in total. However, after G and E take their mortgage amounts, there will not be $100,000 left of the proceeds for F to take. Well, then how is F supposed to get the rest of the money owed? F can sue D personally for the balance. Good luck with that.

7.   Husband and Wife live at Blackacre, Wife's ancestral home for generations. Blackacre has by tradition passed by will to the eldest child of the deceased fee-simple owner, and Wife succeeded to that title upon the death of her Parent. Husband and Wife have Child, now an adult. Husband and Wife divorce. As part of the divorce settlement, Wife gives Husband (all right—soon to be former husband) a life estate in the property. Husband does not record the instrument. Years later, Wife dies, making this question possible.

Wife's will provides that Blackacre passes to Child in fee simple. Child and Husband do not have a good relationship at all, so Child commences an action to evict Husband from Blackacre. Who succeeds?

A. Child wins, because Wife had a reverter interest in Blackacre and willed Blackacre to Child.

Remember to break the alternative down. True or false: Wife had a reverter interest in Blackacre? Certainly she did. She had encumbered her title with Husband's life estate, but had Husband predeceased her, she would once again have had an unencumbered title.

True or false: Wife willed Blackacre to Child?

Yes. So both parts of the alternative are true statements. Does that mean that Child wins? Not in this case.

This is one of the MBE patterns we noted earlier. *See supra* page 18 (1). The "because" statement does *not* cause Child to prevail. Wife did have a right of reversion, but only one thing could bring that right to fruition: Husband's death. While Husband and Wife both lived, Wife still had title to the land, but she had encumbered it with Husband's life estate. Had Husband predeceased Wife, Wife's title would have been unencumbered. Then, upon Wife's death, unencumbered title would have passed to Child. But things did not happen in that order. Wife predeceased Husband. What is the effect of her death? Well, death is usually pretty good at terminating life estates, but almost always it has to be the death of the grantee; death of the grantor does not terminate the life estate, because the grantor's life is rarely the measuring life.[46] So upon Wife's death, what did Child take under the will? Child inherited the title to the land that Wife had upon her death,

---

[46] She could have given Husband a life estate measured by *her* life—an estate *pur autre vie*—but she did not.

but that title was encumbered. An alienee cannot take a greater estate than the alienor had to give, so the life estate went on, and Child inherited the land in fee simple *subject to* the extant life estate. Child cannot evict Husband at any time. (Some may note that this creates a powerful incentive for patricide.)

B.   Husband, because he holds a life tenancy that antedates Child's accession to title.

True or false: Husband holds a life tenancy that antedates Child's accession to title?

This is correct. Wife's death did not snuff out the life tenancy because she did not make hers the measuring life; Husband's life is the one that counts. Child accedes to the title that Wife had at the time of her death. Could Wife, having given Husband a life tenancy (as far as we know without conditions), have evicted Husband during his life? Of course not. Her inability to do so passes to Child together with the fee title.

C.   Child, because Child was not a party to the conferral of the life estate, and Husband never recorded the instrument.

Once again, break the alternative down. True or false: Child was not a party to the conferral of the life estate? Well, that's true, obviously; the question is what effect that has.

If this were a correct answer, think of the principle it would establish for transactions involving life estates. Grantees of life estates could never be certain that the estates would actually survive as long as the grantees did unless all conceivable heirs of the grantor were parties to the instrument. Who are the conceivable heirs of the grantor? Anyone, right?[47] After all, the law does not

---

[47] Since we're talking about concepts, bear in mind that some of grantor's possible heirs may not even have been (pardon the expression) conceived when the grantor created the life estate.

require real property to pass to relatives. Can it possibly be the law that all possible heirs of the grantor must be parties to grantor's conveyance of a life estate?

True or false: Husband never recorded the instrument? True again!

The compound true alternative may be appealing.[48] Recordation, however, only affects the rights of *good-faith purchasers for value*, because recordation allows prospective purchasers to ascertain how good a title they are getting. Recordation does not establish priority for persons who take title to the land without being good-faith purchasers—heirs and donees. Husband had a valid deed. Child was not even entitled to be a party to it, because when Wife created the life estate, Child had no legally cognizable interest in the land. (Child may well have had an expectation, a hope, a wish, a yearning (perhaps even anguish), but the law recognizes none of those.) So this cannot be a correct alternative.

> D. Husband, because when Husband married Wife, they held the land as tenants by the entirety.

True or false: when Husband married Wife, they held the land as tenants by the entirety?

False. Tenancy by the entirety arises only when the spouses take their interest in the property at the same time and by the same instrument. Wife acquired title upon her parent's death, but nothing occurred at that time to vest any title in Husband. It does not matter whether or not Husband and Wife were already married when her parent died. The family tradition was to pass the land by will to the eldest surviving child, which is what Wife's parent did.

---

[48] If you read it fast enough, it will seem more appealing. That's why, when you find an alternative that you think may be the best choice, careful, systematic analysis is all the more important. Part of the purpose of this book is to help you slow yourself down so you will do that sort of analysis.

Husband may have been the parent's son-in-law, but that did not make him the eldest child of the Parent. (For that matter, we should not assume that Husband was older than Wife.) The Parent could, of course, have abandoned the family tradition and provided by will that the land passed to the spouses as tenants by the entirety, but that is not what happened.

8.   Owner held a 700-acre farm in fee simple and leased it to Farmer by written lease from year to year. Farmer had leased the farm for thirty years. In 2020, Farmer planted 500 acres of corn and also had 150 acres of peach orchards that Farmer had planted in the first year of the lease. Farmer died intestate in July, 2020, before any harvesting had begun. Who is entitled to the 2020 crop?[49]

A.   Owner, because Farmer's death terminated the lease, so the land reverted to Owner.

True or false: Farmer's death terminated the lease, so the land reverted to Owner?

First, did Farmer's death terminate the lease? Absolutely. Second, did the land revert to Owner? Of course. Both parts of the alternative are true. But a question still remains: what *is* "the land"? Or, put differently, are both crops part of the land?

This is not a candidate answer. Owner had title to the land, but not to Farmer's personal property. The law recognizes two types of crops: *fructus naturales* (from perennial plants, such as trees) and *fructus industriales* (from annual plants, such as corn or tomatoes). Once established, *fructus naturales* grow naturally, without the aid of people.[50] Trees, grasses, and fruit are *fructus*

---

[49]   Questions do not usually have immaterial facts, so the two kinds of crops should give you a clue to ask yourself what the difference (besides taste) between them is.

[50]   That is not to say that people cannot affect how good a particular year's crop will be by seeing to it that the trees get enough but not too much water, or by fertilizing (unless Don does it). But a peach tree will still be a peach tree next year

naturales. On the other hand, *fructus industrials* require annual planting, cultivation, and fertilizing, so crops like corn, wheat, and beans are *fructus industriales.* The critical difference is that the law views *fructus naturales* as part of the real property until after harvesting, when they become personal property. *Fructus industriales* (also known as emblements) are personal property from the beginning, even when unharvested. Since corn is an emblement, it passes to Farmer's heirs. But the peach crop, because there has been no harvest, is real property and reverts to Owner.

B.   Owner gets the peach crop, but Farmer's heirs get the corn crop.

This is correct. Not all crops are equal under the law of property. Some are part of the real property until harvest; others are the personal property of the rightful possessor of the property from the beginning. In this question, the corn is personal property because it requires annual planting and tending. But the peach trees and their fruit are real property until severed from the land. There has been no severance (harvest), so Owner is entitled to the peach crop. The corn, however, whether harvested or not, is personal property, and since Farmer was the rightful possessor of the property at death, the corn crop passes to Farmer's heirs.

C.   Owner gets all of the crops because there has been no harvest.

True or false: Owner gets all of the crops because there has been no harvest?

This alternative invites you to focus only on the concept of severance, but that concept applies only to structures and to vegetation that survives from year to year without human intervention. Trees, although they may prosper more when aided by

---

without the land possessor doing anything. A corn crop, if the land possessor does nothing after harvest, will be an empty field (except for the weeds).

human intervention, do not need it to survive for more than one year. Other kinds of crops, however, require annual planting and (usually) extensive human intervention. There will still be peaches on the peach trees in 2021, even of no one takes any steps to make that happen. There will not be corn in 2021 unless someone plants it, and that makes all the difference. Annual crops do not require severance to *become* the personal property of the possessor. Perennials, however, do. Therefore, Owner gets the peaches but not the corn.

D.   Farmer's heirs get all the crops.

True or false: Farmer's heirs get all the crops?

Well, this is false. Peaches, you see, grow on trees. Trees are part of the real property, so title to trees (including their leaves and fruit) cannot pass to a lessee until lawful severance from the property. But crops that have only a single-year cycle do not qualify as real property, even before someone harvests them. The upshot is that Farmer's heirs can have corn on the cob for dinner, but they don't get any dessert.

Civil Procedure

1.   Plaintiff sues Defendant in a State A court, alleging a claim for securities fraud within the meaning of the United States Code, which provides a private right of action for securities fraud. Plaintiff seeks $250,000 damages from Defendant. Plaintiff is a citizen of State B. Defendant is a citizen of State A. Defendant timely files a petition removing the action to the United States District Court in State A. Plaintiff moves to remand. The court should:

A.   Grant the motion because Defendant cannot remove an action from the Defendant's state court.

True or false: Defendant cannot remove an action from the Defendant's state court?

This alternative invites you to go too fast. Gee, that removal rule sounds familiar, right? You know you heard it someplace. But it is not right, because the statement is over-inclusive. This alternative ignores an exception to the rule that it states. Defendants cannot remove in-state cases that sound *only* in diversity. They can remove cases where at least one claim qualifies as a federal-question claim, which this claim is. This is not a candidate answer.

B.   Deny the motion on the ground that Plaintiff and Defendant are of diverse citizenship and the amount in controversy is sufficient.

True or false: Plaintiff and Defendant are of diverse citizenship and the amount in controversy is sufficient?

Break the statement apart. Plaintiff and Defendant clearly are citizens of different states. Is the amount in controversy sufficient? Certainly. Finally, does the fact that both parts of the alternative are true lead to denial of the motion? And this is where you should stop short.

This is a federal-question case; the question tells you that the applicable United States Code section creates the cause of action that Plaintiff asserts. *That* is why the court should deny the motion to remand, not because the cases otherwise satisfies the diversity-jurisdiction requirements. The fact that this case satisfies the jurisdiction requirements of the diversity statute is only part of the picture. How did this case get to the federal court? Defendant removed. But as a diversity case, the action is not removable because Defendant is from the forum. (*See* 28 U.S.C. § 1441(b).) Remember that non-federal actions are not removable if *any* defendant is from the forum. This is not a candidate answer, because, as a diversity action, it is not removable.

    C.   Grant the motion because Plaintiff is entitled to choose the forum for trial.

True or false: Plaintiff is entitled to choose the forum for trial?

We hope this alternative didn't even give you pause. If it were true, removal would not exist in any case. Neither would *forum non conveniens* or the federal transfer statutes. This alternative is another vastly overbroad statement; more than that, it is an absolute statement. Absolute statements of rules in alternatives are, if you will, a suspect class. This is not a candidate answer.

Plaintiffs have first choice of forum but not necessarily the last word. Some cases are removable by defendants. Some cases end in dismissal because the court the plaintiff chose lacks subject-matter jurisdiction, personal jurisdiction, or both. Even if the court has both subject-matter and personal jurisdiction, defendant may succeed on a motion to dismiss for *forum non conveniens*.

    D.   Deny the motion on the ground that the case arises under federal law.

True or false: the case arises under federal law?

The question tells you that federal law creates the right of action. It certainly is a federal claim. Congress clearly intended the federal courts to be able to hear such cases. Plaintiff's complaint satisfies the requirements of *Mottley*, *Grable*, and *Gunn v. Minton*. Although the Court has restricted the district courts' subject-matter jurisdiction over the past thirty-five years, it has never denied jurisdiction where a federal statute explicitly creates a right of action.

    2.   Plaintiff sues Defendant in Plaintiff's state's court, seeking tort damages. Defendant properly removes the action to federal

court and, under FED. R. CIV. P. 14, impleads Third-Party Defendant. Plaintiff's state does not allow impleader, though it does recognize causes of action for indemnity and contribution. Third-Party Defendant moves to dismiss Defendant's impleader claim, arguing that state law prohibits Defendant from interposing the claim. The court should:

A.   Grant the motion, because allowing impleader would affect Third-Party Defendant's substantive rights and violate the Rules Enabling Act.

True or false: allowing impleader would affect Third-Party Defendant's substantive rights and violate the Rules Enabling Act?

Once again, let's take it in pieces. Is there a substantive right not to be named as a party? Certainly not! One may prevail in an action, winning on the merits smashingly and getting attorney's fees, but there is no *substantive* right simply not to *be* in an action.[51] What about the second part of the alternative? If there is no substantive right abridged, enlarged, or modified, how can there possibly be a Rules-Enabling-Act violation?

This is not a candidate answer. The *claim* that Defendant asserts against Third-Party Defendant is a valid claim under state law. Conflicting federal and state rules as to *when* and *how* Defendant can assert the claim have no effect on the merits of Defendant's right to recover.

B.   Deny the motion because Rule 14 effects no change in substantive rights, merely acting to accelerate assertion of a substantive right that state law recognizes.

---

[51] Subject-matter jurisdiction and personal jurisdiction rules create, at best, *procedural* rights not to be in an action in a particular court.

True or false: Rule 14 effects no change in substantive rights, merely acting to accelerate assertion of a substantive right that state law recognizes?

This *is* a candidate answer. State law will still control *whether* Defendant is entitled to recover anything from Third-Party Defendant. Federal law in this case only controls *when* Defendant may assert the claim. Rule 14 states no substantive rule of law at all; note that it speaks of two possibilities—that the third-party defendant is *or may be* liable to the third-party plaintiff.

C.   Grant the motion because the state has no impleader procedure.

True or false: the state has no impleader procedure? What did the question say? "Plaintiff's state does not allow impleader. . . ."

This alternative is not a candidate answer. Note the unstated assumption it makes—that state procedural law applies in the federal courts. Now, from time to time that is correct with respect to particular state rules, but it certainly is not generally true. If that were true, there would be nothing for the Federal Rules of Civil Procedure to do.

The existence of impleader is not a substantive-law matter.[52] Impleader is not a claim; it is a procedural device for asserting a claim.

The Federal Rules of Civil Procedure do not march in lockstep with state practice. If they did, there would effectively be 50 versions of the Federal Rules, one for each state. Congress intended there to be uniform procedure in the federal district courts across the country, forbidding the Supreme Court only from establishing

---

[52] Contrast: whether indemnity, comparative negligence, and contribution exist is very much a substantive matter.

rules that abridge, enlarge, or modify substantive state law—the law that determines the merits of claims and defenses.

D. Deny the motion because state law cannot control what happens in federal court.

True or false: state law cannot control what happens in federal court?

You may have a dimly unpleasant memory of *Erie*, but at least the memory is there. And even though what the *Erie* doctrine commands it is not always crystal clear, this alternative is an outrageously overbroad statement that, if true, would entirely undo the doctrine of *Erie Railroad*.[53] State law controls the merits of state-created claims and defenses in the absence of some constitutional violation or a lawful, pre-empting federal statute. This is not a candidate answer.

3. Plaintiff has a million-dollar breach-of-contract action arising out of a contract made and performable in California against Corporation, which has a Delaware charter and maintains its principal place of business in Arizona. Plaintiff brings its action against Corporation in the United States District Court for the District of Arizona. Corporation moves pursuant to FED. R. CIV. P. 12(b)(1) to dismiss the action for lack of subject-matter jurisdiction. The court should:

A. Grant the motion because a corporation cannot be a defendant in a diversity action in a state of which the corporation is a citizen.

True or false: a corporation cannot be a defendant in a diversity action in a state of which the corporation is a citizen?

---

[53] We acknowledge that some students, lawyers, and judges might not regard that as an undesirable result, given the supposed complexity of the doctrine, but *Erie* is nearly one hundred years old and isn't going anywhere.

Stop and think. Yes, you remember something about state citizenship and diversity actions (apart from the complete-diversity rule). But what was it again? Why does diversity jurisdiction exist?

Diversity jurisdiction exists to protect out-of-state parties against possible home-party bias. When personal jurisdiction was sharply restricted—*i.e.* before *International Shoe* changed the jurisdictional landscape—disputes between parties from different states almost always required the plaintiff to commence the action in the defendant's state. That is the prime reason for having diversity jurisdiction. Plaintiff is perfectly at liberty to elect the federal forum in Corporation's state. The limitation that this alternative invites you to misremember is that a defendant from the forum state cannot *remove* a pure diversity action to the federal courts. This is not a candidate answer.

B.   Grant the motion on the ground that the contract and the dispute arising from it have no connection with Arizona.

True or false: the contract and the dispute arising from it have no connection with Arizona?

Well, that's certainly true; there seem to be no Arizona contacts at all for the contract. But when we find ourselves thinking about contacts, what area of the law are we likely to be dealing with? There really are only two possibilities: Civil Procedure and Conflict of Laws. The MBE tests Conflicts only in the context of the *Erie* doctrine. *Erie* is relevant here, but it is clear that federal law cannot govern; the only issue will be *which state's* law will govern each issue. But the question does not ask that, so we're in the realm of Civil Procedure. When we talk about contacts in Civil Procedure, what part of that subject comes to mind? Personal jurisdiction, right? What was the basis for Corporation's motion? It is complaining about lack of *subject-matter* jurisdiction.

This is not a candidate answer. Diversity jurisdiction is a form of subject-matter jurisdiction, not personal jurisdiction. Subject-matter jurisdiction requires no connection of any sort between the underlying claim and the federal forum. There are only two requirements for original diversity jurisdiction: complete diversity of citizenship and the requisite amount in controversy. That the cause of action may have no connection with the forum may supply grounds for a transfer of the case to another federal court, but that does not affect the subject-matter jurisdiction of either the transferor or transferee court.

C.   Grant the motion only if Plaintiff is a citizen of Delaware or Arizona.

True or false: If plaintiff is a citizen of Delaware or Arizona, there is no subject-matter jurisdiction?

This is correct, is it not? The amount in controversy is clearly sufficient, so the only possibility for defeating diversity jurisdiction is lack of complete diversity between opposing parties. Corporations have two citizenship possibilities: their state of incorporation and their principal place of business if that is in a different state. If Plaintiff is a citizen of either state, diversity jurisdiction is impossible. Remember that you can diagram diversity cases using the state citizenships of each of the parties. The diagram for this case looks like: *AZ (or DE) v. DE and AZ.* As soon as you see the same state on both sides of the *v.*, you know that complete diversity does not exist. Therefore, this is a candidate answer.

D.   Deny the motion on the ground that it is always proper to bring an action against a corporation in the federal court where the corporation's principal place of business is.

True or false: is always proper to bring an action against a corporation in the federal court where the corporation's principal place of business is?

As Ronald Reagan said to Jimmy Carter during one of their debates, "There you go again." Before going any further, note that this alternative states an absolute rule of law: "*always* proper." So right away you should be thinking of putting it on the endangered-species list of alternatives.

What part of Civil Procedure does this alternative concern? It talks about the corporation's principal place of business. In fairness, that could refer either to subject-matter or personal jurisdiction. Which is it in this question? Well, it has to be subject-matter jurisdiction, because that's all that the question asks about. And that is why this is not a candidate answer. The stated condition would take care of *personal* jurisdiction, but not subject-matter jurisdiction. An in-state plaintiff cannot properly file in federal court against an in-state corporation a complaint resting only on state law. (Even an out-of-state plaintiff may not be able to file in the federal court; the party alignment would satisfy diversity, but the case must also exceed $75,000, and not every action by an out-of-state plaintiff would.) This is not a candidate answer.

4. Plaintiff, a citizen of New Mexico, sues Defendant$_1$, a citizen of Utah, and Defendant$_2$, a corporation with a Delaware charter and its principal place of business in Idaho. The action is in the United States District Court for the District of New Mexico, seeking $150,000 in damages from defendants for breach of a contract on which defendants are joint obligors. Defendants move to dismiss for lack of subject-matter jurisdiction. What should the court do?

    A. Grant the motion on the ground that a plaintiff cannot bring a diversity action in the plaintiff's own state because the plaintiff has no local prejudice to fear.

True or false: a plaintiff cannot bring a diversity action in the plaintiff's own state because the plaintiff has no local prejudice to fear?

This is a statement of a legal principle that simply does not exist. One can articulate a rationale for it, as this alternative does.[54] But whether it is a good idea or not, there is simply no law—statutory or case law—to support it. Allowing plaintiffs to bring diversity actions in their home states may be more efficient in cases where plaintiffs have every reason to think defendants would remove anyway. It saves the delay and expense of the removal procedure. This is not a candidate answer.

B. Deny the motion on the ground that complete diversity is sufficient and the amount in controversy is sufficient.

True or false: complete diversity is sufficient? Diagram the case using the state citizenships involved: *NM v. UT and DE and ID.* Does the same state pop up on both sides of the *v.*? No. So there is complete diversity.

True or false: the amount in controversy is sufficient?

Correct. Do not be misled by the fact that there are two defendants into thinking that the amount in controversy as to each of them is only $75,000. There are two defendants, but there is only one contract and only one obligation. This is a candidate answer.

C. Grant the motion on the ground that the amount in controversy as to each defendant is only $75,000, which does not meet the jurisdictional requirement for diversity.

True or false: the amount in controversy as to each defendant is only $75,000, which does not meet the jurisdictional requirement for diversity?

---

[54] We can think of an alternative, almost reverse, rationale. If plaintiff is a sufficiently loathsome member of the community, there may be plenty of local prejudice to fear, but it is unlikely to abate simply because the plaintiff elects to sue in federal court. The remedy for that problem is to sue in another state (preferably one far removed from plaintiff's home).

This is the kind of alternative that one is apt to jump at, particularly if hurrying. The math is appealing. The alternative also appeals to people who are trying to figure out how the MBE is out to "get them."

So look closely at what we know about the contract. It is unitary; the two defendants as joint obligors undertook a single obligation to the plaintiff, and the asserted value of that obligation is $150,000. How the defendants may divide up the damage payments if they lose is not part of the case; a plaintiff's judgment will run against both of them. This is not a candidate answer.

D.   Deny the motion on the ground that a diversity action is always proper if plaintiff is diverse from both corporate citizenships.

True or false: a diversity action is always proper if plaintiff is diverse from both corporate citizenships?

We hope the word "always" caused you to sit up and take notice. Can you hypothesize a case where the statement is not true? That's easy in this problem. If Defendant$_1$ were a citizen of New Mexico, the case would satisfy the criterion that this alternative posits, but there clearly would be no diversity jurisdiction.

This is not a candidate answer for two reasons. First, the alternative makes no mention of the required amount in controversy. Second, even if plaintiff is diverse from both corporate citizenships, there may be additional defendants (not in this problem, though) from whom the plaintiff is not diverse. Diversity jurisdiction, except for some class actions and interpleader under the Federal Interpleader Act, requires complete diversity.

5.   A special appearance in a state court or a motion to dismiss for lack of *in personam* personal jurisdiction in a federal court under FED. R. CIV. P. 12(b)(2):

A.   Preserves a defendant's right to attack jurisdiction collaterally following an unfavorable result at trial, provided that defendant limits participation in the litigation to arguing the jurisdictional point and does not otherwise participate in the trial or other proceedings on the merits.

Is this alternative true or false? The first thing to notice is that this is not a question about personal jurisdiction; it is a question about preclusion, specifically issue preclusion. If a defendant objects to jurisdiction in the trial court, and that court denies the defendant's motion to dismiss, can the defendant later ask another court not in the appellate chain from the trial court to overturn the decision on that issue? Then the question looks much easier, doesn't it?

When a defendant contests personal jurisdiction and the forum court decides the issue, its decision on that issue precludes any court other than one in the forum's appellate chain from relitigating the issue. This alternative actually presents the very worst course of action for a defendant, because it surrenders any opportunity ever to litigate the merits in the absence of an appellate reversal on the jurisdiction point. Having lost the jurisdictional issue, the defendant should feel free to contest the merits vigorously; doing so does not insulate the jurisdictional decision from appellate review. This is not a candidate answer.

B.   Preserves a defendant's right to attack jurisdiction collaterally irrespective of defendant's further participation in the forum asserting jurisdiction.

True or false: objecting to personal jurisdiction preserves a defendant's right to attack jurisdiction collaterally irrespective of defendant's further participation in the forum asserting jurisdiction?

This alternative correctly notes that defendant's further participation in the trial court after losing the motion to dismiss is irrelevant, but the principle it states is exactly backwards. The only course of action that preserves the right to attack personal jurisdiction collaterally is to default; then there will be no precluding decision preventing a court in another state from considering the jurisdictional point.[55]

This alternative ignores issue preclusion. A defendant, following a loss on the jurisdictional issue, is free to defend on the merits (and should!) without forfeiting the jurisdictional objection on appeal. This is not a candidate answer.

C. Confines the defendant's financial exposure to the value of defendant's then-owned assets, whether attached or not, at the time that defendant makes the jurisdictional objection.

True or false: by making a jurisdictional objection, the defendant limits financial exposure to assets then owned?

If this rule sounds unfamiliar to you, that's because there is no such rule.

This alternative is wrong for two reasons. First, the judgment in a case founded on *in personam* jurisdiction is not limited to defendant's assets at the time. Judgments have a life span (usually a minimum of ten years), and a plaintiff may recover against defendant's assets throughout the life of the judgment (except for a small category of assets excluded by statute). Second, this

---

[55] Please remember, however, as we're sure you heard in your Civil Procedure course, that defaulting is a very risky way for the defendant to proceed. First, if the defendant has assets in the forum state, the plaintiff can have the judgment executed against those assets. Even if the defendant has no assets in the forum, when the plaintiff does locate the defendant's assets in another state and properly proceeds to have that state's court recognize and enforce the judgment, defendant then *can* attack the trial forum's personal jurisdiction. If the defendant succeeds, great. If the defendant fails, execution will issue, and the defendant will never have an opportunity to contest the merits of the plaintiff's claim. That is the gamble of defaulting.

alternative confuses a special appearance with a *limited* appearance. In a case where the plaintiff proceeds under *quasi in rem* jurisdiction,[56] a limited appearance confines the defendant's exposure to the value of the assets that the court *attached* (no, not all the defendant's assets at that time) to create the *quasi in rem* jurisdiction. (Otherwise the defendant could not defend those assets without risking far greater exposure.[57])

D. Destroys the defendant's right to attack personal jurisdiction collaterally.

True or false: an objection to personal jurisdiction destroys the defendant's right to attack personal jurisdiction collaterally?

You bet! The general rule of preclusion, whether claim or issue, is that a party gets one bite at the apple, plus whatever appeals may lie from an unsuccessful bite. This is not a question about jurisdiction at all; it is a question about issue preclusion. If the forum court decides the jurisdictional issue, only an appellate reversal can displace that determination.

QUESTIONS ## 6-10 REFER TO THE FACT PATTERN BELOW, WITH MODIFICATIONS AS INDICATED.

Plaintiff sued Defendant, seeking damages for Defendant's alleged negligence resulting in an automobile accident in Virginia. Plaintiff is a citizen of Maryland; Defendant is a citizen of North Carolina. Plaintiff commenced the action in the United States District Court for the District of Virginia, seeking $50,000 for personal injuries and property damage suffered in the accident. Plaintiff included in the complaint a claim for defamation, alleging

---

[56] Yes, *quasi in rem* jurisdiction still exists after *Shaffer v. Heitner*; it just requires more contacts in many cases than it used to.

[57] That may have been part of the Court's discomfort in *Shaffer*. Delaware law forbade limited appearances, so out-of-state defendants faced the undesirable choice of (a) defaulting, and losing the attached or sequestered property, or (b) appearing to defend the property but in the process exposing themselves to potential liability far in excess of the attached property's value.

that one month before the accident, Defendant had given a lecture at the University of Virginia asserting that Plaintiff was incompetent in Plaintiff's profession. On that claim, Plaintiff sought $60,000 damages. Defendant moved to dismiss the action for lack of personal jurisdiction. Virginia has a long-arm statute that explicitly goes to the constitutional limits and is one of the four states that still adheres to contributory-negligence doctrine. After briefing and argument, the district court (whether correctly or not in your view) granted the motion. Plaintiff did not appeal. Plaintiff then filed the same two causes of action in the proper state trial court in Virginia.

6.   Was plaintiff's complaint in the federal action defective for joinder of the negligence claim with the completely unrelated defamation claim?

    A.   Yes, because joinder of totally unrelated claims unnecessarily complicates trials, taking excessive amounts of judicial time and confusing juries, thus diminishing defendants' entitlement to effective jury trials.

True or false: joinder of totally unrelated claims unnecessarily complicates trials, taking excessive amounts of judicial time and confusing juries, thus diminishing defendants' entitlement to effective jury trials?

You know, there is a lot of sense in that. Multiple causes of action, especially if unrelated, can extend the length of trials and may confuse juries. But there is a remedy for that; under Rule 42, the court can order the claims severed for separate trials. And even if the possibility of severance did not exist, what you need to be thinking about is not whether the alternative states a policy that makes sense, but rather what the Federal Rules of Civil Procedure actually say.[58]

This is not a candidate answer. No federal pleading is defective because of joinder of multiple claims; Rule 18 allows unrestricted joinder of claims. Remember, though, that the fact that parties can join multiple claims without committing a pleading error says nothing about whether the court will have either subject-matter jurisdiction with respect to any of the claims or personal jurisdiction over any of the defendants. All Rule 18 says is that it is not a *pleading* defect (as it was at common law) to join different types of claims.[59]

B. No, because the Federal Rules of Civil Procedure permit joinder by a party of as many claims as the party has against another party, irrespective of the claims' relationship or lack of relationship with each other.

True or false? We hope this sounds familiar to you, because the alternative is a direct paraphrase of Rule 18. Therefore, this is a candidate answer.

C. Even if joinder was proper, the court should have dismissed the action *sua sponte* for lack of subject-matter jurisdiction.

True or false? The first thing to note is that the first two alternatives dealt with the rules of joinder, but this one concerns subject-matter jurisdiction. Well, is there anything wrong with this alternative? That is, is there a problem with subject-matter jurisdiction here?

---

[58] This sentence may suggest to you that some of the Federal Rules may make no sense (and we might agree). But that doesn't matter; the only criterion for the validity of a Federal Rule of Civil Procedure is whether it violates the Rules Enabling Act by trenching on substantive matters.

[59] Repeat after us: no Federal Rule of Civil Procedure has any effect on the rules of subject-matter or personal jurisdiction. Keep repeating it.

Let's diagram the case using the states' postal designations, including what we know about the claims.

MD v. NC (defamation $60,000, and negligence $50,000)

There clearly is no ground for federal-question jurisdiction here, so we must consider diversity. Does the party lineup satisfy the requirement of complete diversity? Sure. So if there is a problem, it must lie with the amount-in-controversy requirement.

This alternative invites you to think that each claim in a pure diversity action must surpass the jurisdictional floor of $75,000. That is not so. For purposes of satisfying the amount-in-controversy requirement, a party can aggregate the amounts of multiple claims against an opposing party. Things get more complicated if there are multiple opposing parties, but with only a plaintiff and a defendant, the rule is clear. This is not a candidate answer.

D.   No, provided that Virginia law permits such joinder, because in a diversity case presenting no federal issues, state law governs joinder of claims.

True or false: state law governs joinder in diversity actions?

Aw, c'mon! Even if you got no sleep the last two nights, you should nail this one. Joinder is purely a matter of procedure, so state law cannot displace the governing federal rule. The Federal Rules of Civil Procedure always apply in the federal courts unless they violate the Rules Enabling Act, and the Supreme Court has never declared that any of them does.[60] This is not a candidate answer.

---

[60] Consider the unlikelihood of the Court ever doing that. It is, after all, the body that promulgates the rules. (It may occur some day, however. There is precedent; remember that in *Erie R. Co. v. Tompkins,* the Court declared its own behavior (and the lower federal courts' under the Washington All-Stars' direction) over the 96 years since *Swift v. Tyson* unconstitutional. (But the 96-year period for the Federal Rules of Civil Procedure will not expire until 2034.))

7. Is Plaintiff's state action subject to dismissal by reason of principles of claim preclusion?

   A. No, because there is no predicate judgment on the merits of Plaintiff's claims.

True or false: there is no predicate judgment on the merits of Plaintiff's claims?

That's true, isn't it? The federal court dismissed on jurisdictional grounds. Claim preclusion requires a (1) valid, (2) final, (3) judgment on the *merits* of a claim. The federal court never addressed the merits.

   B. Yes, because Plaintiff is not entitled to bring another action on the same claims.

True or false: Plaintiff is not entitled to bring another action on the same claims?

Although the statement has an intuitive appeal, it also states an absolute rule. Is it true that a plaintiff gets one and only one chance to sue? That is far too broad; Plaintiff is entitled to a judgment on the merits absent a forfeiture of the claims under the statute of limitations. Jurisdictional dismissals do not invalidate claims; the dismissals merely limit the forum in which the plaintiff may pursue the claims. This is not a candidate answer.

   C. No, because the decision of the federal court has no effect other than as persuasive precedent on the courts of the state.

True or false: the decision of the federal court has no effect other than as persuasive precedent on the courts of the state?

This is a tougher alternative to evaluate because it may remind you of two provisions of law that do not apply here. First, you may think of the Full Faith and Credit Clause of the Constitution. That's fine, but you need to recall that the Clause addresses only the effect that *state* courts must give to other states' courts judgments. It does not address the federal courts at all. Second, you may then recall the Full Faith and Credit Act, which does address the federal courts. Unfortunately, it speaks only *to* the federal courts, telling them that they must give full faith and credit to judgments of state courts. It says nothing about what state courts should do when confronted with federal judgments.

This alternative is not a candidate answer. State courts accord preclusive effect to federal judgments. Neither the Full-Faith-and-Credit Clause nor the Full-Faith-and-Credit Act requires that result, but all states do apply their principles of preclusion to federal decisions even though there is no federal law requiring them to do so.

> D.   Yes, because the federal decision establishes that Virginia cannot exercise jurisdiction over Defendant.

True or false: the federal decision establishes that Virginia cannot exercise jurisdiction over Defendant?

If you are thinking about the law of preclusion, you will recognize this as a true statement, but your work is not done at that point. You must also remember the call of the question, which asks if *claim* preclusion prevents the second action. It does not, because there is no valid, final, judgment *on the merits*; the judgment was procedural. So this is not a candidate answer.

> 8.   Is Plaintiff's state action subject to dismissal by reason of principles of issue preclusion?
>
> A.   No, because there is no predicate judgment on the merits of Plaintiff's claims.

True or false: there is no predicate judgment on the merits of Plaintiff's claims? Absolutely true. Now, does issue preclusion *require* a preceding valid, final, judgment on the *merits* of Plaintiff's claims? And this is where (and why) you should slow down.

This is not a candidate answer, because issue preclusion requires only a (1) valid, (2) final, (3) decision on the merits of *the particular issue*, **not** on the claim or case as a whole, provided that the decision on the issue was essential to the judgment. So note what this alternative does by implication. It says that there is no issue preclusion in the absence of a merits disposition of at least one claim. Jurisdiction is the area that makes that implied statement not true.

B.   Yes, because Plaintiff is not entitled to bring another action on the same claims.

True or false: Plaintiff is not entitled to bring another action on the same claims? The only correct answer to that question is, "It depends." On what does it depend? It depends on whether there has been a judgment on the merits of the claims and whether the statute of limitations has run.

Although this alternative may have a certain intuitive appeal, Plaintiff is entitled to a judgment on the merits absent a forfeiture under the statute of limitations. Jurisdictional dismissals do not invalidate claims; the dismissals merely limit the forum in which the plaintiff may pursue the claims. This is not a candidate answer.

C.   No, because the decision of the federal court has no effect other than as persuasive precedent on the courts of the state.

True or false: Federal judgments have no binding effect on subsequent state proceedings?

That is a false statement. State courts accord preclusive effect to decisions of federal courts. Neither the Full-Faith-and-Credit Clause nor the Full-Faith-and-Credit Act requires that result, but all states do apply their principles of preclusion to federal decisions even though there is no federal law requiring them to do so.[61]

D.   Yes, because the federal decision establishes that Virginia cannot exercise jurisdiction over Defendant.

True or false: the federal decision establishes that Virginia cannot exercise jurisdiction over Defendant?

This statement is correct. This question tests your understanding of principles of personal jurisdiction, issue preclusion, and the *Erie* doctrine. Recall that absent a federal statute dealing with personal jurisdiction (as in 28 U.S.C. § 2361 (one of the three statutes constituting the Federal Interpleader Act)), the federal courts use the personal jurisdiction rules of the states in which they sit. Here the federal court determined that the Constitution did not permit Virginia to exercise personal jurisdiction even under the state's all-encompassing long-arm statute. Now, that decision was certainly wrong, but that does not allow Plaintiff to relitigate it in another court. Plaintiff's remedy for an incorrect jurisdictional dismissal lay in the appellate process—appeal to the Fourth Circuit—not in a collateral attack.

MODIFICATION # 1:

Suppose that in the original (federal) action, Plaintiff had not joined the defamation claim. In this variation, the federal court denied Defendant's motion to dismiss on personal jurisdiction grounds but dismissed *sua sponte* for lack of subject-matter jurisdiction. Plaintiff then brought the negligence claim in a North Carolina state court. North Carolina has adopted the Federal Rules of Civil

---

[61]   It's not hard to figure out why states do this. If they did not, they would be saddling their own, already overcrowded judicial dockets with retrying issues that a federal court tried and fully determined. That would be remarkably inefficient.

Procedure as its own rules of procedure in state-court actions.

9. If the North Carolina negligence action ended with a judgment on the merits for Plaintiff, and Plaintiff later sued on the defamation claim in another North Carolina action, would principles of claim preclusion require dismissal of the defamation action?

    A. Yes, because claim preclusion requires Plaintiff to have joined all then-existing claims and now operates to require dismissal of any claim that was or might have been joined.

True or false: claim preclusion requires a claimant[62] to have joined all then-existing claims and now operates to require dismissal of any claim that was or might have been joined?

Note what we have here—another absolute statement of law. What language makes it absolute?

Claim preclusion requires joinder of all *transactionally related* claims, not of all existing claims. The preclusion doctrines exist to promote efficiency in use of judicial and litigant resources. Claim preclusion prevents parties from splitting claims, and the majority approach requires joinder of transactionally related claims only. Joining unrelated claims does not produce much efficiency. This is not a candidate answer.

    B. No, because claim preclusion does not require joinder of claims that are not transactionally related.

True or false: claim preclusion does not require joinder of claims that are not transactionally related?

---

[62] We generalize from "plaintiff" to "claimant" here because claim preclusion principles govern successive claims by any party to litigation, whether the party is a plaintiff, defendant, third-party defendant, or intervenor.

This is a correct statement. More than that, it is a rule of law that actually makes sense![63] There are few, if any efficiencies from joining such claims, and the presence of unrelated claims in a single case may make the action more difficult to try and actually produce inefficiency. So this is a candidate answer.

C.   Yes, if Plaintiff could have joined the defamation claim with the negligence claim in the federal court.

True or false: Claim preclusion requires dismissal if Plaintiff could have joined the defamation claim with the negligence claim in the federal court?

Let's break this one down, even though the alternative is not a compound statement. First, *could* plaintiff have joined the two claims in the federal court? What Rule governs the permissibility of joining claims. Well, that's Rule 18. Does Rule 18 *demand* joinder of multiple claims?

Rule 18 permits, but does not require, joinder of any claims.[64] It does not require joinder even of transactionally related claims. Federal preclusion law, not any of the Federal Rules, requires joinder only of transactionally related claims. So, yes, Plaintiff could have joined the defamation claim with the negligence claim,[65] but there was no rule of law compelling that joinder.

D.   No, because claim preclusion never operates where there is no valid, final, judgment on the merits on the theory of recovery in Plaintiff's second complaint.

True or false: claim preclusion *never* operates where there is no valid, final, judgment on the merits on the theory of recovery in Plaintiff's second complaint?

---

[63]   Most of them do, but, as you doubtless have discovered, not all of them.

[64]   FED. R. CIV. P. 18(a) (emphasis added): "A party asserting claim, counterclaim, crossclaim, or third-party claim *may* join. . . ."

[65]   Plaintiff did so in the unmodified version of this question.

Why do you think we emphasized that word? There you go! It makes an absolute statement. We have not done a systematic study of MBE questions with respect to this, but we strongly suspect that when a question writer puts in an absolute term like that, the writer is issuing an invitation to students to forget some exception to the otherwise general rule.

This is where you need to have read and considered the alternative very carefully. This alternative is a subtle misstatement of claim-preclusion doctrine. The correct test is transactional relationship, not theory of recovery. Thus, if after an automobile collision a plaintiff sues for assault and battery from the defendant's handling of the automobile and loses, the plaintiff cannot then file a second action seeking recovery for the accident on a negligence theory. The plaintiff could have joined a negligence count in the first complaint but cannot have saved it as a fallback for additional litigation. This is not a candidate answer.

MODIFICATION # 2:

> Suppose that the negligence action had gone forward in the North Carolina court, as in Modification # 1. Suppose also that Defendant had prevailed, the jury returning a special verdict finding Defendant not to have been negligent and Plaintiff to have been negligent. Now, Defendant commences an action against Plaintiff in Virginia federal court to recover for extensive crash damage to Defendant's $250,000 antique Rolls Royce Silver Shadow.

10. If Defendant moves for summary judgment on the issue of liability, and Plaintiff moves to dismiss Defendant's claim under Rule 12(b)(6) on the ground that Defendant did not interpose the negligence claim properly, how should the court view the competing motions?

A.   Neither motion has a sound basis.

True or false: neither motion has a sound basis?

Let's consider this in pieces. What must be the basis for Defendant's summary-judgment motion? Clearly the finding in A-1 that Plaintiff was negligent, right? Since Defendant seeks issue preclusion, think about the criteria for issue preclusion. Does Defendant meet all of the criteria?

Did the parties actually litigate the issue of Plaintiff's negligence? Sure. Did the jury actually decide the issue of Plaintiff's negligence? Check. Anything else? Oh, yes, was the decision on that issue essential to the judgment? Suppose instead the jury had not found Plaintiff negligent. Who would have prevailed in A-1? Well, since the jury found Defendant not negligent, Defendant would have prevailed in A-1 anyway.

Let's change it around. Suppose instead the jury had not found Defendant free from negligence. Who would have prevailed in A-1? Well, since the jury did find Plaintiff to have been negligent, and Virginia is a contributory-negligence jurisdiction, Defendant would have prevailed in A-1 anyway.

So in the actual case, neither jury finding gets preclusive effect because neither was essential to the judgment.[66] Therefore, there is no sound basis for Defendant's motion.

---

[66] In effect, therefore, where the issues independently caused the result in the earlier litigation, the courts treat the decisions on the issues as if they were gratuitous. Where the original action required the combined effect of multiple issue decisions to cause the result, all of those issues qualify for issue preclusion.

Here is an example of the difference, based on the contributory- (not comparative-) negligence model. (The majority (and MBE) rule is comparative negligence unless a specific question instructs you differently, but we want this example to be as clear as possible.)

(A-1)   *A v. B* (damages) (automobile collision)

The jury returns a special verdict, finding A to have been negligent and B not to have been negligent. B wins. Each of those issue decisions fully explains B's verdict. Under the majority approach, neither would get issue preclusive effect in subsequent

Now look at Plaintiff's 12(b)(6) motion. What could Plaintiff's counsel have been thinking? Defendant's complaint obviously states a claim; it is the reciprocal of Plaintiff's complaint in A-1. And that should cause alarms bells to go off.

Defendant states a claim, but that is not all of what Rule 12(b)(6) talks about. It must be a claim "upon which relief may be granted." Why might Defendant's claim fail that part of the test? Whenever you see a problem with successive cases, you should begin thinking about preclusion, not least because questions testing substantive knowledge do not need successive cases to set them up. What do we know about North Carolina law? We know one thing with certainty. North Carolina has adopted the FRCP as its own procedural code. Why might there be preclusion of Defendant's action? And now the principle of Rule 13(a)—not the Rule number necessarily—should come to mind. Defendant's claim, arising as it did from the same transaction or occurrence as Plaintiff's claim, was a compulsory counterclaim, yet Defendant did not file the claim. So there clearly is a sound basis for Plaintiff's 12(b)(6) motion because of that. This is not a candidate answer.

> B.   Defendant's Rule-56 motion is correct, but the court should deny Plaintiff's motion because there has been no litigation of Plaintiff's possible liability to Defendant.

True or false: Defendant's Rule-56 motion is correct?

Alternately stated, is Defendant entitled to preclusion on the issue of Plaintiff's negligence? No. Under the majority approach,

---

litigation, because either decision alone fully explains why B prevailed. Neither decision, considered independently, is essential to the A-1 judgment.

Suppose instead this litigation:

(A-2)   *A v. B* (damages) (automobile collision)

The jury returns a special verdict, finding A not to have been negligent and B to have been negligent. A wins. Neither of those decisions *independently* fully explains A's verdict. For A to prevail, *both* decisions had to go A's way. Both were essential to the judgment. Both get preclusive effect.

Plaintiff may be able to relitigate the negligence issues because the decision on *either* negligence issue in the first case fully supports the judgment for Defendant, without the other issue. So without going further, we know that this alternative is not a candidate answer.

But we are going to go further,[67] even though you need not. True or false: there has been no litigation of Plaintiff's possible liability to Defendant? Well, yes and no. The first action did litigate the issue of Plaintiff's negligence, but the jury made no finding of Defendant's liability to Plaintiff. In this the jury was correct; that issue was not before it. But look what that this part of the alternative would do: it would destroy the idea of compulsory counterclaims entirely. In this case, one of the issues that Defendant's action relies upon was litigated, but none of the others were. Does that prevent the compulsory-counterclaim rule from operating? Suppose Defendant had a plausible, transactionally related counterclaim that did not contain an issue from the first case. Does that render the counterclaim permissive?

Let's make this more real. Suppose that Defendant's claim in the second action sounded not in negligence but in assault and battery—Defendant alleges that Plaintiff ran into Defendant's vehicle deliberately. Was that a compulsory claim? (Please say, "Yes.") And yet, there clearly are issues, such as Plaintiff's intent, that the first action did not litigate. For the court to deny Plaintiff's motion on this basis would eviscerate Rule 13(a).

    C.   There may be arguable basis for the Rule-56 motion in some states, but the court should dismiss the action in response to Plaintiff's motion.

True or false: there may be arguable basis for the Rule-56 motion in some states?

---

[67] By this time, that should not come as a shock to you.

Not all states follow the majority rule with respect to issue preclusion when multiple issue decisions from the first action independently support the judgment. In those states, Defendant would get preclusion on the issue of Plaintiff's negligence.

True or false: the court should dismiss the action in response to Plaintiff's motion?

The property-damage claim was a compulsory counterclaim in the first action. Defendant has forfeited it. Defendant's Rule-56 motion, though it goes against the majority approach, would be meritorious in minority-approach states, but that would not save the action from dismissal.

D.   Don was not able to think of a fourth plausible alternative for this question, so this is not a candidate answer. Don't choose it.

Evidence

1.   Plaintiff sues Defendant for injuries Plaintiff suffered when Defendant's car collided with Plaintiff when Plaintiff stepped off a sidewalk curb preparatory to crossing the street. Police arrived at the scene and took statements from both parties and several witnesses, noting the statements in the police report. Plaintiff confided to an officer that Plaintiff had had several beers in the hour before the accident. At trial, Plaintiff testified that Plaintiff had been minding Plaintiff's own business, waiting for the traffic light to change, when Defendant's car hit Plaintiff as Plaintiff stood in the street next to the curb. On cross-examination, Plaintiff denied being intoxicated at the time of the accident. Defendant subsequently called as a witness the police officer who took Plaintiff's post-accident statement. Defense counsel asked the officer whether the officer had taken any statement from

Plaintiff relating to alcoholic beverages or other intoxicants and, if so, what Plaintiff had said. Plaintiff's counsel objected to the question as calling for hearsay. How should the court rule?

A.   The officer cannot testify about what Plaintiff said to the officer if the defense is offering the statement to prove that Plaintiff was intoxicated; it is inadmissible hearsay.

True or false: offering the statement to prove that Plaintiff was intoxicated is impermissible because the statement is hearsay?

Plaintiff is a party to the action. Plaintiff's statement to the officer is not hearsay at all under the Federal Rules of Evidence. It is an admission. Statements by parties are not hearsay because the parties are available for cross-examination. This is not a candidate answer.

B.   The officer can testify what Plaintiff told the officer because Plaintiff's statement is a declaration against interest.

True or false: what Plaintiff told the officer because Plaintiff's statement is a declaration against interest?

Does Plaintiff's statement potentially harm Plaintiff's case? Well sure it does; otherwise the defense would not be trying to get it in. This is where the difference between colloquial usage and legal usage is critical. "Declaration against interest" is a term of art, and it has a specific meaning and specific requirements.

The declaration-against-interest[68] exception (FRE 804) applies only (1) when the declarant is unavailable; (2) the statement is

---

[68] Please do not make the mistake of thinking of Plaintiff's statement as an "*admission* against interest." That phrase improperly conflates different bases for admitting evidence, and the different bases have different supporting rationales. (Think about it; virtually every admission that the opposing party seeks to introduce is against the interest of the party making the statement. Why else would the opposing party want to introduce it?)

contrary to the declarant's pecuniary, proprietary, or penal interest, and (3) was so when declarant made the statement. Plaintiff has testified at trial and so clearly is available. Plaintiff's statement satisfies the second and third criteria, but two out of three isn't good enough under 804. This is not a candidate answer.

C.   The officer cannot testify what Plaintiff told the officer because the defense can introduce the police report as a business record, and it is the best evidence of what Plaintiff said.

True or false: the defense can introduce the police report as a business record? It is true that the report can come in as a business record *if properly authenticated.*

True or false: it is the best evidence of what Plaintiff said?

This part of the alternative invites you to glom onto an expression you have heard—best evidence (rule)—and to choose it reflexively. Since we are trying to dull your reflexes, stop and think for a second. When does the best-evidence rule come into play? It applies when the original of a document is not available and counsel seeks to introduce evidence of the contents of the document through testimony or by using a copy of the document.[69] But that's not the case here. Here defense counsel simply wants the officer to testify what the officer heard when Plaintiff spoke to the officer. That statement is either inadmissible or admissible regardless of whether the officer made notes and regardless whether any notes qualify as a business record. This is not a candidate answer.

D.   The officer can testify what Plaintiff said to the officer because it is an admission, and therefore not hearsay.

---

[69] This follows the common-law and common-sense notion that the document itself is the best evidence of what the document says. The common-law rule has faded as a literal statement, because it is easy to introduce a copy of an original document that is no longer available, provided that there is proper authentication of the copy.

True or false: Plaintiff's statement to the officer is an admission?

What is an admission? It is a statement by a party-opponent. Please note: an admission most often is damaging to the party-opponent, but it need not be.

True or false: an admission is not hearsay?

Correct. FRE 801(d)(2) says explicitly that the statement of a party (that meets several criteria, all of which this situation satisfies) is not hearsay at all. This is a candidate answer.

2.   Counsel calls Witness to the stand and asks Witness if Witness spoke with Declarant on the day in question. Witness answers, saying, "Yes, I spoke with Declarant on Monday, March 20, and Declarant said that there was a blizzard in Rochester." Declarant died between March 20 and the trial. Opposing counsel objects and moves to strike the answer as hearsay. How should the court rule?

CRITICAL NOTE: Let's get something out of the way at the beginning. At this point, it is not possible to answer the question at all. You cannot characterize any statement as hearsay or non-hearsay unless you know the purpose behind offering the statement—what the statement is supposed to prove. Out-of-court statements are often admissible for one purpose but not for others.

A.   The court should sustain the objection because Declarant is not available for cross-examination, making Declarant's statement hearsay.

True or false: Declarant's unavailability for cross-examination makes Declarant's statement hearsay?

This is true-false question is, in some sense, a trick. What makes it a trick? It is not answerable because you still don't have enough information to answer intelligently. This alternative *assumes* that counsel asked the question for the purpose of establishing what the weather was in Rochester on March 20, but the facts do not indicate that. There are other reasons for asking the question, and Declarant's response may be admissible to prove things other than what the weather was in Rochester. This is not a candidate answer.

    B.   The court should overrule the objection if counsel argues that the purpose of the question was to show that Declarant was alive on March 20.

True or false: the court should overrule the objection if counsel argues that the purpose of the question was to show that Declarant was alive on March 20?

Begin, as always, with the definition of the legal term that the question involves. What is hearsay? Hearsay is an out-of-court statement by someone other than the witness now testifying that is offered to prove the truth of the contents of the declarant's statement.

Did counsel offer Declarant's statement to show that it was snowing in Rochester on March 20? Not at all; counsel offered the statement to demonstrate that Declarant was still alive on that date (which could, for example, be important in some disputes over estates, where if the Declarant predeceased the testator, one set of people would share in the estate, but if testator predeceased Declarant a different set of people would share).

By contrast, if counsel had offered the statement to show what the weather in Rochester was on March 20, it would have been hearsay and inadmissible.

But if counsel offers the statement to show that Declarant was alive at the time (or that Declarant and Witness were acquaintances, for example) it is not hearsay and is perfectly admissible. The *content* of Declarant's statement is irrelevant.

Think of it this way: if counsel asked Witness simply whether Witness had spoken with Declarant on March 20, would the question be subject to a hearsay objection? Clearly not. What Declarant said is irrelevant; what is important is that Declarant spoke.[70] Therefore, this is a candidate answer.

C.   The court should sustain the objection if counsel argues that the purpose of the question was to show that Declarant was in Rochester on March 20.

True or false: the court should sustain the objection if counsel argues that the purpose of the question was to show that Declarant was in Rochester on March 20?

You need to be careful here. It is tempting to think that Declarant must have been in Rochester to comment on the weather. But that's not true, is it? There are many sources of weather information besides looking out the window. Besides, Declarant may have had no knowledge of what the weather in Rochester was; perhaps Declarant just made it up. The statement says nothing about where Declarant was. Declarant may have been in Singapore for all the court knows. Even if the statement was that Declarant was in Rochester, then it is being offered to show the truth of the matter asserted: Declarant's location. That makes it inadmissible hearsay. This is not a candidate answer.

D.   The court should overrule the objection, in its discretion, because the court can take judicial notice of what the Rochester weather was.

True or false: the court can take judicial notice of what the weather in Rochester was on March 20?

Really? How does the court know what Rochester weather was on March 20? What is the court's source of knowledge about that?

---

[70] Sex identification to one side, does "dead men tell no tales" sound familiar?

Even if the court happens to know (perhaps March 20 was the judge's birthday and the judge happened to be in Rochester that day), then is judicial notice permissible?

Before you jump too quickly, would not the judge then be acting as a witness rather than as a judge? In the world of litigation, that is known as a "no-no." Judges do not get to play dual roles in trials. Judicial notice has a very limited scope. Courts can take notice of indisputable facts, *e.g.* that March 20 on the year in question fell on a Tuesday, but they cannot take judicial notice when facts are disputable. "Blizzard" is an uncertain term. Perhaps it was just a snow flurry, and Declarant panicked. Perhaps it snowed quite hard, but the weather had been so warm the week before (in Rochester??) that the snow melted almost as soon as it touched the ground. This is not a candidate answer.

QUESTIONS ## 3-8 REFER TO THE FACT PATTERN BELOW.

Defendant met Victim, an acquaintance, one summer evening. They went out for a drink, and returned to Defendant's apartment. Neighbors heard loud noises and called the police, who found Victim dead on the kitchen floor with a knife in Victim's chest. Apparently in shock, Defendant admitted killing Victim, but claimed Victim threatened to kill Defendant, approached in a menacing manner, and finally cornered Defendant in the kitchen, where Defendant killed Victim in self-defense. The district attorney charged Defendant with Victim's murder. At Defendant's trial, the prosecutor offers in evidence an opened envelope postmarked a week before Victim's death, discovered when the police searched Defendant's apartment. The envelope contained a handwritten letter signed "Victim" stating that Defendant owed Victim money. The letter threatened to mail several lewd photos of Defendant to a sleazy magazine unless Defendant repaid the debt. The prosecution authenticated the letter.

3.   Is the letter admissible?[71]

   A.   Yes, to prove that Defendant owed Victim money and to prove Victim's threats to mail lewd photos to a magazine.

True or false: the letter is admissible to prove its own assertions?

This is classic hearsay, isn't it? The contents of the letter cannot come into evidence for their truth. If the letter never existed, and Defendant were to testify that, "Victim said to me that I owed Victim money and that Victim would cause me great embarrassment if I did not pay," would that testimony from the Defendant be admissible to show that the Defendant actually owed Victim money?[72] Of course not! Well, that result doesn't change just because the out-of-court statement is written rather than oral. This is not a candidate answer.

   B.   Yes, to prove Defendant's motive to kill Victim.

True or false: the letter is admissible to prove Defendant's motive to kill Victim?

This is a candidate answer. The letter says what it says, whether or not the representations are true. If the jury is willing to infer that Defendant opened *and read* the letter,[73] then it is relevant. The inferences the jury might draw from the letter may be weak, and the jury need give the letter no weight at all, but that does not affect its admissibility. This is not a candidate answer.

   C.   No, because the letter is hearsay.

---

[71]   *See supra* page 148: CRITICAL NOTE.

[72]   Of course, nothing would stop counsel examining Defendant from simply asking Defendant whether Defendant owed Victim money. That evidence would be admissible, because then it is the witness's (Defendant's) own statement rather than the written statement of an out-of-court declarant offered for the truth of its assertion.

[73]   Note that there is no direct evidence that Defendant either opened or read it, although the police found it open in Defendant's apartment.

True or false: the letter is hearsay?[74]

At this point, the true/false question is unanswerable; it *cannot* be a candidate alternative. Why? Because nothing in this part of the question gives any indication of the purpose for which the prosecution is offering the letter. It may be hearsay; it may not. There is no way to tell. If the prosecution is offering the letter to prove that Defendant owed Victim money, that is improper— offering the letter to prove the truth of its contents. But if the prosecution is offering the letter so that the jury may infer that reading the letter might have given Defendant a motive to take action to avoid the threats the letter contained, then it is admissible.

> D.   No, because the letter is testimonial and violates Defendant's constitutional right of confrontation.

True or false: the letter is testimonial?

This is not a candidate answer. If you think the letter is testimonial, stop and ask yourself what testimony the letter is giving. Then you will notice that the letter is testimonial only with respect to the things it asserts. If the prosecution is not offering the letter to prove that Defendant owed Victim money or that Victim possessed compromising photographs of Defendant, then the letter is not testimonial.

True or false: if the letter were testimonial (that is, if the prosecution were offering it to prove the debt's or the photographs' existence), then admitting it in evidence would violate Defendant's constitutional right of confrontation?

The Supreme Court has been less than pellucid in this area, but if the letter is testimonial, and the Declarant is not present at trial,

---

[74] *See supra* page 148: CRITICAL NOTE.

and Defendant never had a prior opportunity to cross-examine Declarant, then the statement is almost certainly correct.

4.   The prosecutor calls Friend, who has known Defendant for years and is quite fond of Defendant. The prosecutor asks Friend about a conversation with Defendant one week before Victim's death. According to Friend, during the conversation Defendant stated to Friend, "Victim has been hassling and threatening me. Victim had better stop it or I'll make Victim sorry." Should the judge allow Friend's testimony?

A.   Yes, because it is an admission.

True or false: Defendant's statement to Friend is an admission?

Certainly it is. It is a statement by a party, and the opposing party seeks to introduce it. Defendant's statement is an admission of possible motive (and perhaps intent). The inference that Defendant contemplated murder is weak because the statement is not sufficiently specific, but that goes to the weight of the statement, not to its admissibility. This is a candidate answer.

B.   Yes, because it proves Defendant's state of mind.

True or false: Defendant's statement proves Defendant's state of mind?

Alas, no. Perhaps it proves Defendant's state of mind seven days before the killing, but that is not the state of mind that counts for the prosecution. Defendant's state of mind *at the time of the killing* is quite relevant because it may affect whether the jury finds that Defendant was properly acting in self-defense, or did not intend to kill but rather merely to defend, or did intend to kill but is eligible for conviction of manslaughter only, or fully intended to kill and did not qualify for voluntary manslaughter. But that is not the state of mind to which Defendant's statement to Friend concerns. This is not a candidate answer.

C. No, because it is hearsay not within any exception.

True or false: Defendant's statement it is hearsay not within any exception?

It is a statement by a party. Statements by parties cannot be hearsay unless the party is not available for cross-examination. Defendant is sitting in the courtroom. That is not to say that Defendant may not have a difficult choice to make. If Defendant chooses to testify (either to deny ever having made the statement or to explain its meaning), that is a waiver of the Fifth Amendment privilege. But this alternative cannot be a candidate answer because statements by parties that opposing parties offer in evidence are not hearsay at all under the Federal Rules of Evidence. This is not a candidate answer.

D. No, because the statement is testimonial and violates Defendant's right of confrontation.

There may be issues of whether Defendant ever said such a thing or what Defendant meant by saying it. But whose statement is it? It is Defendant's own statement. Friend is available for cross-examination, so that is not a problem. Defendant is in court. Defendant can testify. This is not a candidate answer.

5. Defendant takes the witness stand and seeks to testify that during the time Defendant was acquainted with Victim, Defendant heard from acquaintances that Victim on three separate occasions within the past four years viciously assaulted persons, the first occasion with a tire iron, the second occasion with a knife, and the third occasion with a hammer. Should the judge allow this testimony?[75]

A. Yes, to prove Victim's character for violence.

---

[75] *See supra* page 148: CRITICAL NOTE.

True or false: the testimony is admissible to prove Victim's character for violence?

Please do not indulge the knee-jerk answer that the "owner" of the character must first put character in issue. That is true with respect to a defendant in a criminal case. It is not true with respect to the victim. Evidence of Victim's character is admissible if it bears specifically on the crime charged. Other things being equal, Victim's character for violence is provable.

But there is a different problem here. The out-of-court statements of "acquaintances" are being offered to prove the truth of the matter asserted. The acquaintances are not available for cross-examination, and Defendant is not offering testimony of Victim's general reputation in the community. The statements are hearsay, and there is no applicable exception. This is not a candidate answer.

B.   Yes, to prove Defendant's fear of Victim.

True or false: the testimony is admissible to prove Defendant's fear of Victim?

This is where you must be careful. The truth of the statements the acquaintances made is irrelevant if the purpose of the offer is to show that Defendant had reason to fear Victim, which in turn bears on Defendant's possible state of mind at the time of the killing. That is permissible. Defendant is testifying about what Defendant heard about Victim. Doesn't that permit the jury to make an inference (even if a weak one) about Defendant's mental state? This is a candidate answer.

The prosecution can cross-examine whether anyone ever did say that, who said it, on what occasion, etc. The prosecution can cross-examine on whether Defendant has the same trait. The prosecution can also rebut by introducing independent evidence about the victim's character.

C. No, because the proof is hearsay and not within any exception.

True or false: the proof is hearsay and not within any exception?

Once again, this alternative does not specify why Defendant is offering the testimony.[76] It may be a really attractive alternative, but it is not correct. To think this alternative is correct, you must *assume* the purpose for which Defendant offers the testimony, but in this alternative, you do not know. *If* Defendant offers the evidence to show that Defendant had reason to think Victim was violent, which in turn bears on Defendant's state of mind at the time of the killing, then it is not hearsay; so this cannot be a candidate answer.

D. No, because proof of other crimes is only admissible if there is a proper purpose and there is no proper purpose for this proof.

True or false: proof of other crimes is only admissible if there is a proper purpose? Well certainly that's true. Proof of *anything* is only admissible if there is a proper purpose. In addition, there is nothing to indicate that those incidents, even if they did occur, resulted in criminal charges at all, much less in conviction.

True or false: there is no proper purpose for this proof?

Why is Defendant offering this proof? What do the contents of the acquaintances statements concern? They are not convictions; they are alleged prior bad acts relevant to Defendant's (not Victim's) actions. Prior bad acts are admissible as evidence for some purposes, but they are not admissible to show propensity. Is there any proper purpose for this proof? Well, it is relevant to show that Defendant had *reason to think* that Victim might be violent. Note

---

[76] *See supra* page 148: CRITICAL NOTE.

the distinction here; the proof is not admissible to show that Victim *was* a violent person, but it is admissible to show that Defendant had reason to believe that Victim was. Purpose is everything. This is not a candidate answer.

6. Following Defendant's direct examination, the prosecutor seeks to cross-examine Defendant about Defendant's conviction eight years earlier for possession of a forged driver's license, a misdemeanor. Defense counsel objects. How should the court rule?

   A. Not admissible. The prejudice from introducing the conviction substantially outweighs its probative value.

True or false: the prejudice from introducing the conviction substantially outweighs its probative value?

Let's start at the beginning. What is the probative value of the evidence? Does it tend to show that Defendant murdered Victim? Of course not.

What about prejudice? What is the possible prejudice to Defendant if this evidence comes in? What does it tend to show? It tends to show that Defendant is not always honest, so it tends to impeach Defendant's credibility. Is it permissible for attorneys to try to impeach the credibility of opposing witnesses?

Finally, is Defendant's earlier possession of a forged driver's license so prejudicial that it greatly outweighs its tendency to show that Defendant is not always honest?

Impeachment to attack the witness's credibility is permissible. The question is whether this conviction is usable in that way. The prosecution is not offering it as evidence of Defendant's character, but rather as evidence that Defendant may be untruthful. Misdemeanor convictions bearing on truthfulness are admissible if within F.R.E. 609's 10-year time limit, and there is no balancing test. The fact that there is no balancing test is a fairly good clue that the F.R.E.'s perspective is that a misdemeanor conviction cannot rise to the level of being unduly prejudicial. This is not a candidate answer.

B.   Admissible. The possible prejudice from introducing the conviction does not outweigh its probative value.

True or false: the possible prejudice from introducing the conviction does not outweigh its probative value?

This alternative asks you to make a value judgment. Some questions do ask for balancing, but this is not one of them. The evidence of the forged-license conviction is not likely to cause the jury to believe that Defendant committed murder, but it is likely to cause the jury to question whether Defendant is believable. And so this answer may appear tempting, since both the result and the explanation are true. Careful! What is the rule with respect to introducing misdemeanor convictions? FRE 609(a)(2) makes clear that there is no applicable balancing test, in contrast with Rule 609(a)(1). So this alternative is not a candidate answer even though it arrives at the right result, because it includes as part of the reasoning a balancing test that does not exist in the applicable rule.

C.   Not admissible. The conviction is for a misdemeanor, not a felony.

True or false: The Federal Rules of Evidence do not allow introduction of misdemeanor convictions for any purpose? The alternative does not say that explicitly, of course, but that is the only theory that could underlie such a broad statement.

FRE 609(a)(2) allows misdemeanor convictions bearing on credibility to come into evidence as long as they occurred within the preceding 10-years. This is not a candidate answer.

D.   Admissible, without balancing probative value and prejudice.

This is correct. The prior conviction bears on truthfulness. Because it is a misdemeanor, there is no balancing.

7.   Defendant calls Better Friend[77] to testify that BF has known Defendant for fifteen years and to describe numerous occasions when Defendant tried to break up fights and settle verbal disputes and arguments. Should the judge allow BF's testimony?

  A.   No, because BF is giving his opinion, and not testifying as to Defendant's reputation.

True or false: BF is giving his opinion?

Is BF expressing an opinion at all? Clearly not; as described, BF is offering evidence of prior good acts by Defendant. Leave to one side the question of whether prior good acts may be evidence; as soon as you recognize that BF is not offering an opinion of any sort, this part of the alternative (and therefore the entire compound conjunctive alternative) cannot be correct.

BF is entitled to give BF's opinion about Defendant's character, and that opinion may rest at least in part on the incidents described. The old common-law rule about only reputation (and not opinion) evidence no longer is true. As long as the witness has a sufficient basis for having an opinion, the evidence comes in for whatever it is worth.[78]

True or false: BF is not testifying as to Defendant's reputation?

That, at least, is true. BF does not even purport to be testifying about Defendant's character or reputation for character in the

---

[77] Friend who originally testified may have been Defendant's BFF. No longer.

[78] "For what it is worth" is a phrase you may hear from judges, usually in non-jury trials, when they are curious about what a witness was going to say before counsel objected. Don was in that situation once in the Southern District of New York. Don's adversary asked a witness a question that clearly called for hearsay. Don objected. The judge said she would take it "for what it is worth." Don felt like saying, "I just explained to you that it isn't worth anything." He didn't.

community. But that true part of the alternative cannot save the whole. This is not a candidate answer.

> B.   No, because BF's testimony is not in the proper form in which to give character testimony.

True or false: BF's testimony is not in the proper form in which to give character testimony?

This one is pretty easy. BF is saying nothing directly about Defendant's character. The defense may want the jury to infer that Defendant is not a violent person based on the prior good acts to which BF is testifying, but those are not proper bases for the jury to make an inference about Defendant's character. Character for evidence purposes is a matter of one of two things, either character in the community (which may know nothing of Defendant's prior good acts) or the opinion of the witness, provided that there is a sufficient foundation for the witness to have an opinion. The long-standing acquaintanceship of BF and Defendant plus BF's having observed many prior good acts may well provide a basis for BF to express an opinion. But BF is not stating an opinion here.[79]

> C.   Yes, because BF has known Defendant for a sufficient amount of time to give reliable character testimony.

True or false: BF has known Defendant for a sufficient amount of time to give reliable character testimony?

Fifteen years is certainly long enough, but that is not the problem here. This is not a candidate, though you may find it tempting. Although the "because" statement is true, the testimony is not in proper form. BF is entitled to state an opinion with respect

---

[79]   If you begin to sense that defense counsel asked the wrong questions, you are on the right track. As this question relates it, counsel has not laid a proper foundation for BF's opinion evidence. Counsel should explore the length and nature of BF's acquaintanceship with Defendant to establish BF's entitlement to have an opinion about Defendant's character. Then counsel may ask BF on what BF bases that favorable opinion. At that point, and not before, BF can testify how BF came to be of the good opinion of Defendant's character that BF now has.

to Defendant's character but not simply to describe all the wonderful things Defendant has done.

D.   Yes, because Defendant placed character in issue.

True or false: Defendant placed character in issue?

This one depends on how you look at it. One might say that Defendant has not placed character in issue because counsel intends to ask questions that do not go directly either to character or to BF's expressing an opinion about Defendant's character. On the other hand, one might say that Defendant is obviously attempting to place character in issue. In fact, it doesn't matter which of these is true.

The placed-character-in-issue formulation is not relevant here; it's a test of when the *prosecution* can introduce character evidence relating to Defendant. The prosecution isn't taking the initiative here; Defendant is. But the evidence still must be in proper form, and a witness's litany of Defendant's prior good acts is not proper form. BF can testify that BF's opinion is that Defendant is a peace-loving and non-violent person. The prosecution can then cross-examine to explore the basis for BF's opinion, and in response to the prosecutor's questions, BF may mention prior good acts, but not until then. This is not a candidate answer.

8.   In rebuttal, the prosecutor seeks to prove through Co-Worker, who worked with Victim in a travel agency for two months, that Victim was an easygoing and non-violent person. Should the judge allow Co-Worker's testimony?

A.   Yes, because character testimony is always admissible in a homicide case.

True or false: character testimony is always admissible in a homicide case?

Here is another absolute statement of law, and therefore it is highly suspect right off the bat. It is a considerable overstatement. The prosecution cannot introduce character evidence relating to either the Victim or Defendant unless Defendant opens the door. This is not a candidate answer.

B.   No, because positive character proof about a victim is not admissible unless the victim's character is first attacked by negative character testimony.

True or false: positive character proof about a victim is not admissible unless the victim's character is first attacked by negative character testimony?

This alternative is really appealing, but it is incorrect because it is too specific. What is it that makes it too specific? The expression "negative *character* testimony" is not accurate. Under FRE 404(a)(2)(C), prosecutors can offer trait evidence to rebut evidence that the victim was the aggressor, but the evidence that the victim was the aggressor need not only be "negative *character* testimony"; the evidence of victim's aggression may, for example, be circumstantial, or it may even come from a witness who asserts that the witness saw the victim attack the defendant. Co-Worker's testimony, if otherwise allowable, might tend to impeach the witness. This is not a candidate answer.

C.   Yes, because Defendant opened the door by attempting to prove that Defendant acted in self-defense.

True or false: Defendant opened the door by attempting to prove that Defendant acted in self-defense?

This is a candidate answer. Defendant introduced evidence (Defendant's testimony) tending to show that Victim was the aggressor. Under FRE 404(a)(2)(C), the prosecution is entitled to rebut and may do so by introducing evidence of Victim's generally non-violent character.

D.   No, because knowing somebody for two months is never enough time to enable a witness to provide trustworthy character evidence.

True or false: knowing somebody for two months is never enough time to enable a witness to provide trustworthy character evidence?

There certainly is no part of the Federal Rules that articulates this or any other time requirement, and it is not a judgment that you are qualified to make in the abstract. And you need not attempt it.

This may be a tempting alternative, but a moment's pause should remind you that the short period of acquaintanceship goes only to the *weight* of Co-Worker's testimony. Whether the evidence is trustworthy is a matter for the jury. Defendant can cross-examine to try to impeach Co-Worker's testimony on that basis, but it does not make the testimony inadmissible. This is not a candidate answer.

9.   Plaintiff suffered severe injuries when a train struck Plaintiff's pick-up truck at a grade-crossing. Plaintiff sues Railroad, claiming the engineer was driving too fast for conditions and that Railroad improperly maintained the crossing, creating an unreasonably dangerous situation. Railroad denies both claims, asserting that Town (in which the crossing is), not Railroad, is responsible for maintaining the crossing. Plaintiff offers evidence that, shortly after the accident, Railroad put up gates at the crossing. The Railroad objects to this evidence. The evidence is:

A.   Admissible as relevant to the dangerousness of the crossing at the time of the accident.

True or false: the evidence is admissible as relevant to the dangerousness of the crossing at the time of the accident?

Ah, Torts. You may feel a certain nostalgia for first year, when "all" you had to worry about was your course load, not an entire bar examination. What does this alternative really ask about? Isn't it whether Plaintiff can use Railroad's subsequent action, in effect, as an admission-by-action that not having gates was negligent? But, that is the one thing that Railroad's post-accident actions are *not* relevant to show. Post-event repairs are not admissible to show negligence. The policy underlying this rule is that we don't want to discourage alleged tortfeasors from making necessary repairs, and allowing such evidence to come in would discourage them from doing so or at least delay the repairs until after the case ended. This is not a candidate answer.

    B.   Inadmissible; subsequent repairs are inadmissible to show negligence.

True or false: subsequent repairs are inadmissible to show negligence?

That statement is quite true; that's one of the things upon which you spent some class time in Torts.

True or false: the evidence is therefore inadmissible?

Note the unspoken assumption of this part of the alternative: that there can be one and only one possible use for this evidence. But that is not so, is it? The same piece of evidence can affect more than one issue in a case. If Railroad had no control over the maintenance of the grade crossing, can the crossing's possibly shabby state of repair demonstrate Railroad's negligence? Evidence of subsequent repairs, while certainly not admissible to show negligence, *is* admissible to show control of the site. Whether careful instruction by the judge in charging the jury is sufficient to prevent the jury from tasting the forbidden fruit is, of course, questionable, but the law at least pretends that it is. This is not a candidate answer.

C.   Admissible as relevant to the question of Railroad's control of the intersection.

True or false: the evidence is admissible on the issue of whether Railroad controlled the grade crossing?

This is correct. The evidence should come in subject to an instruction from the court to the jury that the evidence cannot show that Railroad negligently maintained the crossing but can show, if the jury is willing to make the inference, that Railroad *controlled* the crossing. Then the Railroad's argument that maintenance was Town's responsibility (with the inference that Railroad therefore was not entitled to maintain the crossing) is subject to question.

D.   Inadmissible for all purposes to encourage persons to correct dangerous situations without fear of increasing their exposure to liability.

The policy of encouragement is accurate, but the result is not. Repair connotes control. In this case it rebuts Railroad's defense that only Town is responsible for maintaining the crossing. The law of evidence strikes a balance in refusing the evidence for purposes of showing negligence but allowing it to show control. You may think it would be a better world if the rule were all encompassing. Perhaps it would be, but there is a balancing going on, and each of the three possibilities (admissible for all purposes, admissible only to show control, inadmissible for all purposes) comes with a cost. This is not a candidate answer.

10. Plaintiff sues Defendant for injuries received when Plaintiff fell down the stairs in Defendant's store. As EMTs were removing Plaintiff from the store on a stretcher, Floor Manager came over and said, "I'm really sorry you fell. I wasn't there but it must have been something left on the stairs." At trial, Plaintiff's counsel asks Plaintiff, "What did Floor Manager say

to you as you were leaving the store on a stretcher?" Defendant objects: The statement should be:

A. Excluded, because it is prejudicial, and the prejudice outweighs the probative value of the testimony.

True or false: the Floor Manager's statement is prejudicial in a way that outweighs the testimony's probative value?

This is not a candidate. In some sense, all evidence offered against a party's position is prejudicial. So what? The problem here is different. There is no foundation for the testimony—nothing to show that Floor Manager has any knowledge—and there is nothing to weigh. The statement itself undercuts any prejudicial effect. We wouldn't let anyone else testify that there must have been something on the stairs unless that person had observed it personally. Why should the floor manager be any different? The statement admits that it is pure speculation.

Here's another way to think of it. Suppose, as the EMTs carried Plaintiff across the sidewalk, a Passer-By asked Plaintiff what happened, and Plaintiff replied that Plaintiff had fallen down the stairs. If Passer-By said, "It must have been something left on the stairs," would that statement be admissible to prove that there was indeed something on the stairs? Of course not; Passer-By has no clue what actually happened. Well, neither does Floor Manager; the only difference is that Passer-By was outside the store and Floor Manager was within. Neither has any personal knowledge of whether there was anything on the stairs. This is not a candidate answer.

B. Excluded because Floor Manager, even if a person authorized to be a speaking agent for defendant, needs personal knowledge.

True or false: Floor Manager, even if a person authorized to be a speaking agent for defendant, needs personal knowledge?

That's true of every witness whose testimony tends to establish or rebut an element of a claim or defense, isn't it? Being floor manager does not make Floor Manager a seer. Floor Manager admits it is speculation, not even asserting that there *was* something on the stairs. This is a candidate answer.

C   Admitted, because it is a statement against interest.

True or false: Floor Manager's statement is a statement against interest?

"Statement against interest" is a non-existent category. There are admissions (statements by parties or by persons authorized to speak for them), and there are declarations against interest (out-of-court statements that would be inadmissible hearsay but for the fact that the unlikelihood of the Declarant making the statement falsely is low enough that the law allows the evidence to come in if the Declarant is unavailable as a witness). So right away, this cannot be a candidate.

Floor Manager's statement is neither an admission nor a declaration against interest, because the manager makes clear the absence of personal knowledge; the statement is pure speculation.

D.   Admitted even though Floor Manager lacks personal knowledge because the statement is within the scope of Floor Manager's employment.

True or false: the statement is within the scope of Floor Manager's employment?

It may be within Floor Manager's scope of employment to make statements on behalf of Defendant, but it is not within Floor Manager's scope of employment to make statements not based on personal knowledge. This is not a candidate answer.

11.   Defendant puts Witness on the stand to testify about a meeting Witness attended. Witness attempts to name the other persons

at the meeting but has forgotten some of them. Defense counsel gives Witness a memorandum properly marked for identification and establishes that Witness wrote the memorandum (which includes a list of who was present at the meeting) immediately after the meeting. Witness recalls writing the memorandum and is sure it was accurate when written, but "this was a long time ago and I just don't remember now who was present at the meeting." The attorney offers the memorandum in evidence. Plaintiff objects. The court should:

A.   Exclude the memorandum because the jury may only hear someone read the memorandum.

True or false: the jury may only hear someone read the memorandum?

This is a tricky area that falls under FRE 803(5). The memorandum is only admissible *as a document* if an adverse party offers it. Here Defendant called Witness, so only Plaintiff can get the document itself admitted in evidence. However, Defendant, having established a proper foundation, can ask Witness to read the memorandum to the jury. This is not a candidate answer.

B.   Admit the memorandum because it is a business record.

True or false: the memorandum is a business record?

Note for future attorneys: not every thing that an employee writes during the work day—even if it relates to the business— qualifies as a business record. This memorandum does not satisfy at least two of the elements of the business-record exception: (1) there is nothing to indicate that making and retaining this kind of employee memorandum was the regular practice of the business (or even of the employee), and (2) there is nothing to indicate that the meeting that Witness attended was a regularly conducted activity of the business. Now, take one more step back. Is there anything in the facts to suggest that there was any business operating or, if there was, that Witness was an employee of that business? There is no foundation for treating Witness's memorandum as a business record under FRE 803(6). This is not a candidate answer.

> C. Exclude the memorandum because it has not been authenticated.

True or false: the memorandum has not been authenticated?

Of course it's been authenticated; Witness remembers writing it and vouches for its accuracy. That doesn't make the memorandum gospel; opposing counsel can certainly cross-examine to try to undermine the *weight* the jury should accord the document when its contents are read, but that does not go to the permissibility of reading the memorandum into the record. Note, though, that the mere fact that Witness authenticated the memorandum still does not make it a business record. This is not a candidate answer.

> D. Not excluded because the memorandum is past recollection recorded.

True or false: the memorandum is past recollection recorded?

News flash: "past recollection recorded" is not a dirty phrase. Pasting that (accurate) label on the memorandum does not make it inadmissible. FRE 803(5) allows past recollection recorded to be evidence, provided that counsel seeking to use the evidence introduces it in the proper manner and establishes a solid foundation. *But,* in this case, the memorandum *document* cannot come into evidence unless Plaintiff introduces it. The best Defendant can get is to have Witness read the memorandum to the jury.

12. Plaintiff and Defendant were involved in a car accident. A grand jury indicted Defendant for driving while impaired. Witness testified before the grand jury that Defendant was driving normally at the time, but the grand jury nonetheless

indicted. Defendant pleaded guilty as charged, and the court fined Defendant $1,000. After the plea and sentence, Plaintiff sued Defendant for negligence, seeking damages for personal injury. In that action, Witness testifies for Plaintiff that Defendant was driving on the wrong side of the road. On cross-examination, Defendant seeks to question Witness about Witness's grand jury testimony.

Plaintiff's attorney objects. The court should rule that Witness's statement before the grand jury is:

A. Admissible for impeachment only.

True or false: Witness's grand jury testimony is admissible only for impeachment?

Tempting, perhaps, but not so. FRE 613 allows prior inconsistent statements in trials or grand jury proceedings to come in as having independent testimonial value. This is not a candidate answer.

B. Admissible as its truth only.

True or false: Witness's grand jury testimony is admissible only for its truth?

If you chose this answer, you should be at least mildly embarrassed. It is easier to use evidence for impeachment than to get it admitted as proof of a material fact. In this case, Witness has made a prior inconsistent statement. That goes to Witness's credibility and so it is admissible also to impeach. This is not a candidate answer.

C. Admissible for both impeachment and for its truth as substantive evidence.

This is correct under FRE 613.

D. Inadmissible because it is hearsay not covered by an exception.

˙True or false: Witness's grand jury testimony is hearsay not covered by an exception?

There really are two problems with this alternative. First, a prior inconsistent statement by a witness is admissible for impeachment purposes even if it is otherwise hearsay. The issue will be whether it is admissible also for the truth of its contents. Second, it's the declarant's own statement, and declarant is subject to cross-examination. This qualifies as a witness's prior statement under FRE 613.

Epilogue

No one said this would be easy. But it will be effective. Passing the MBE does not require brilliance, an eidetic memory, or 16-hour days. All it requires is patience, perseverance, and practice. There is a fourth "p" that will also be helpful: a partner. Practicing on your own is great, but having a partner to discuss the material with adds a critical dimension. As the two of you work things out, your understanding will deepen, and your confidence and comfort level will rise.

As we have said all along, at the beginning it will be slow, but as you get into each subject, you may be surprised at how much quicker your mind gets in a relatively short time. This is really all about technique, not fund of knowledge. Practice taking questions and alternatives apart and dealing with them piece by piece. The *gestalt* approach does not work at all well in legal analysis. Breaking everything down does.

Do remember that it is often the case that slower is faster. By going more slowly at the beginning, you cement the technique and lay the groundwork for moving more rapidly without being careless in your reading or thinking. That's where practicing with a partner really pays off. The best way to increase your own understanding of a principle or doctrine is often to teach it to someone else—someone who can ask intelligent questions when you seem to have skipped a step or two or just have not been quite precise enough in your explanation.

We hate clichés like the plague, but this is not rocket science. (One might view it as brain surgery, but without the scalpel.) You are teaching your brain to approach multiple-choice questions differently. It is similar to the process we all went through in our first year of law school—training our brains to work in the way lawyers' brains need to work. You did it then. Now, with those three or four years of experience behind you, you are in a much better position to tweak the skills you have learned so they work even better for you on this particular type of examination.

You can do it. Be patient with yourself.